Meant For You

Paula Ion

Copyright © 2024 by Paula Ion

All rights reserved.

No portion of this book may be reproduced in any form without written permission from the publisher or author, except as permitted by U.S. copyright law.

Contents

PROLOGUE.	1
CHAPTER ONE.	4
CHAPTER TWO.	12
CHAPTER THREE	20
CHAPTER FOUR	29
CHAPTER FIVE.	38
CHAPTER SIX	49
CHAPTER SEVEN	59
CHAPTER EIGHT	68
Chapter Nine	74
Chapter Ten	80
Chapter Eleven	88
Chapter Twelve.	95
Chapter Thirteen	104
Chapter Fourteen	112

PROLOGUE.

✱ Third Pov*

(Trigger warning)

TERRIFIED. She was terrified. Her frantic pants and abnormally racing heart were all over the place. And she knew without a doubt that trouble was brimming. She could practically feel it grinding her body.

God, please don't let him come in here. Please! Please! Please!. She silently pleaded.

She was trembling with fear now. The footsteps were getting closer.

No no no no.

She quickly glanced at the side window from under the table, where she was hiding. She wished her small body would give her the courage to fly out the window. She needed to cry for help. She didn't want this. She didn't want any of this.

At just 12 years and a few months old, Sansa had learnt the harsh ways of life. The rejection from her dad who she yearned to feel his love, the pain of watching her mother die right in front of her eyes, seeing how her dad beat her mother relentlessly to death.

And now, trying to so desperately to escape the clutches of her wicked cousin. Godwin was 3 years older than her. And he was a spoiled, rotten kid.

"Sansa..?"

Sansa slightly whimpered as she heard that dreadful voice. She placed her tiny hands over her softly bitten lips. He was upstairs now. The door was opened, which meant he was already in the room. She curled her toes and held her knees as tightly as possible, as the fear gripped her.

"Sansa...? Come out now, before I loose my patience!" He whispered in a grave, taunting voice. His voice sounded too harsh for a boy at that age.

Sansa kept quiet. Her full, long hair covering her face, making it difficult for her to make out anything in the dark room. But Sansa didn't care. All she wanted was to escape. Daddy! Where are you!

She screamed as the predator instantly got hold of her arm from above the table, dragging her roughly out of her hiding place.

Before she could catch herself, she was being flung to the other side of the room with a loud crash into to waste basket.

Sansa wasn't aware of the aching pain that bursted out on her side. She was still screaming. Her eyes moved fearfully around the room, searching for a weapon, anything to protect herself with.

"Leave me alone! I will tell my daddy!" Sansa screamed, the fierce anger of a brave little girl. She waved a rubber slipper in front of him. Like it could protect her.

"Your daddy cannot save you. Not this time princess. Come... Let me show you something." He replied with an amused chuckle.

Sansa's small head bobbed back and forth. She gulped as her evil cousin began unzipping his Jean trouser, his lips wide with the harshest smile Sansa had ever seen on anyone's face.

"No..... Please....."

****

SANSA OSAZE is a beautiful young girl who has had a terrifying past filled with violence, abuse and dark secrets which threatens to override her sanity.

Things change for the better when her scholarship Application to one of the most prestigious tertiary institutions located at Abuja, Nigeria, gets miraculously accepted.

Sansa is ecstatic as she finds this as an opportunity to escape her mean father.

Sansa then, decides to give her terrible life a new, fresh start. She starts to believe that she might actually have a normal, regular life.

UNTIL... She meets Richard, who like her, has so many dark secrets and an overly guarded heart.

Eventually, One thing led to the other and before either of them knew what was happening, Hatred became undeniable passion.

They were meant for each other, but the world wanted them apart.

CHAPTER ONE.

✶ Sansa* (Pov)

MY EYES SCANNED THE WHOLE ROOM FOR THE UMPTEENTH TIME. Complete. Set to leave this prison of a house.

My body could hardly contain the excitement that was flowing ceaselessly through me. It still felt like a dream. Leaving this house. Leaving this hell hole.

I was brought out of my trance by a soft knock on the door, followed by a slight push as Aliu, our butler, peeped in. His dark, bald head shinning against the bright lightened room.

"Excuse me, Madam Sansana, I wanted to inform you that the cab driver has arrived."

"Alright. Thank you, Aliu. I'll be downstairs in a minute." I replied with a soft smile at the man that even though he was employed as our butler, I'd taken him as my friend and confidant over the years. I would miss him dearly.

"Oh and... Madam Sansana?"

I chuckled lightly at the way he always mentioned my name. "Yes... Aliu?"

"Your father is downstairs as well. Waiting for you."

I nodded tightly at his words. I knew I was going to have that last confrontation with the devil. Yes, my dad.

I noticed Aliu's eyes scan the room which was filled and scattered with boxes and traveling bags. He was probably wondering why I had so many load.

"I'll start moving your boxes to the car now, Madam." He said as he proceeded to pick up one of the heaviest boxes.

"Oh, no.. Don't worry about it, Aliu. I can-"

"Ah-Ah, no. It is my job and I must do it."

"But-"

"No buts, Sansana. Please, do not stop me."

I smiled warmly at him. Aliu was one hardworking man. From overseeing the kitchen, to arranging my father's busy schedules and watching over the mansion. He was always so eager to work.

"Thank you, Aliu."

He bowed slightly as a form of reply and moved to carry the boxes out.

I turned and went forward to stare at myself in my large mirror. I would miss my mirror. It was as wide as the wall of my room. So much so that you could see every other parts of the room.

I stared at myself for a while. I'd singlehandedly braided my long, stubborn hair into a large fish tail, which brought out the details of my face.

My large smokey eyes fringed with long dark lashes, the angle of my straight, pointed nose, my high cheek bones which made me look almost mean, and finally my chin. It had a dent in the middle, making my chin look more protruding.

I was wearing one of my favorite outfits today. A pink sweatshirt, dark green shorts and a white sneaker. Looking at me in public, one would think I was much more older than the 19 year old that I am. Since I was young, I'd been having that rapid growth.

My breasts were a little larger than the average, which made my stance look more defiant and matured. And then, my wide hips, so much like my mom. My mom....

I sighed and smiled brightly at my self in the mirror. No pasts. No regrets. No pain. No remembrance.

MR COLLINS OSE OSAZE WAS SEATED BEHIND HIS DESK as I pushed open the door without even knocking.

His head speedily snapped up first in fear, then surprise at seeing me. I hardly entered his office to talk him. I hardly even communicated with him in this big house.

"Adesua, my daughter, you're leaving early?"

I felt my face scrunch up in anger. He knew how much I hated being called that name. I preferred Sansa. Even though I could never understand what pushed my mother to give me that odd name, I would always prefer it to Adesua, the one my father gave me. It just didn't sit well with me.

"Yes, Father. There are some documents I have to sign immediately before my lectures starts. And I have to go over my profile information to make sure I don't forfeit my scholarship."

My Father dropped his face down with a stressed sigh. "In the next 10 years to come, I will never understand why you choose to leave Lagos, where there are better private schools, to go to Abuja. Where you've never even been to!"

"I prefer to go there because I worked towards it! I don't need your own meddling hands in my affairs anymore. I'd prefer to work my butt off by myself than have you do it for me with your bloody money!"

"You will not use such tone with me, young lady!"

"Oh, don't worry. I won't even use any tone with you once I'm out of here for life!"

I saw his eyes widen and glisten with unshed tears. It didn't move me. Not even a bit.

"You will never forgive me for what I did to your mother." He said in a tiny, broken voice.

"Leave mom out of this!"

"For goodness sake, Sansa, What happened was a mistake! I've begged and begged for forgiveness! Even Your mom in heaven would have forgiven me by now!"

I just couldn't help it. I bursted into hard feats of laughter in front of my father. My body was trembling with the force of my laughter.

"You're just so unbelievable, Mr Collins. I have no time for your terrible attempt at reconciliation. Good bye, dad." I said and turned to walk out.

"I love you, Sansa." He said.

I froze and slowly turned back to him. Love? Love?!

"I hate you." I replied. I heard the gasps outside and knew for a fact that the servants were steadily listening to our conversation. Rude people.

"Be careful, Sansa. Watch what you say to me. I am your father."

"A father who killed my mother!"

"It wasn't intentional! Jesus!"

"You were never remorseful! You kept me locked up and didn't even allow me to attend my own mother's burial! You never listened to me! Never attended to me! You destroyed my life! Now you talk about love because I'm leaving..?!"

By the time I had finished venting out, My father had already left his seat behind the desk and was walking towards me. I noticed the tears had already escaped. I didn't think he noticed. My father detested crying.

"I won't banter words with you, my daughter. I just want you to take this." I looked down at what was on his hands. I was about to swat his hand off before my eyes caught the picture.

I instantly froze the moment I saw my mother's beautiful face and.... Me. She was holding me in her arms. Little me. I felt my eyes unconsciously water as I stared at the picture.

"Why are you showing me this now?" I tried to sound harsh, but I knew my voice came out in a miserable squeak.

"I have always wanted to give it to you."

"Thank you." I croaked out.

And then I felt it. His warm, flat lips on my forehead. The tears I'd been trying so hard to keep at bay finally fell off the moment I shut my eyelids.

I felt his tall, strong frame move with a strong tremor and I knew he was crying. Crying for what? I didn't know. But I cried along with him.

We held each other for what seemed like hours, before I awkwardly pulled back and angled my head up so I could stare at him.

"I have put enough money into all of your accounts. And I've contacted your aunt at Abuja. When you feel like you need to lay off campus.. You can go spend time with her. She'll gladly welcome you with open arms."

"Uh, no. I've had enough of family members. And besides... I'm sharing an apartment off campus with another student."

"But still... Her contact and address has been sent to your mail." He countered with a stern look. I glared back at him. Then he broke into a smile.

"Take care of yourself, my stubborn girl." He said.

****

I SIGHED WITH DELIGHT AS I FELT THE FRESH AIR OF ABUJA WAVE THROUGH ME. I Squealed in delight as we approached the school gates. I smiled as I read the bold writing in front of the gate.

GENTRY UNIVERSITY.

I still couldn't believe that I was going to be schooling in one of the most prestigious schools in Africa. Their facilities was topnotch.

According to my research, they were one of the schools that aimed on giving students a quality education that was up to the British standards. The cost of attending the school without a scholarship was at least half the price of sending a student to study abroad currently.

The school gate was over 6km from Abuja central Area, On Jabi airport road bypassing ring road. The social area and sports complex was also as wide as an average national stadium.

Gentry University began in April 2009 with a foundation class and just three faculties. Currently, they have about seven faculties with their different facilities.

The school itself was originated by a sole proprietor. I wasn't able to find any information about the man so that was all I knew.

"We're here, Ma'am." The driver said, making me break out of my thoughts.

"Oh, Thank you!" I replied enthusiastically and jumped out of the car with the boxes I could manage to carry.

AFTER ABOUT AN HOUR, all my things were stacked into the tiny but sturdy apartment. I was wondering why my roommate, Amarachi Ekezie, wasn't around yet. She was supposed to arrive earlier than me.

After I paid the cab man and plugged my phone into my charger, I quickly dashed to the toilet to ease myself.

When I returned to the room, I started sorting out my things; books, clothes, cutleries and some furnitures. I scanned the tiny room and smiled the moment I realized I was finally free. Freedom.

I was about to begin the arrangements of my furnitures when I distantly heard the scrapping sound of heels on tiles.

"SANSA OSAZE!! OH MY GOD! I'M SO EXCITED TO FINALLY MEET YOU!!" I placed my hand over my head with a wince as my new room mate walked in. She was practically screaming.

"Hi, Amarachi, I'm....."

I trailed off as my eyes landed on her. Woah.

She was wearing an almost see-through bra or bikini, I could practically see the dark crests of her nipple. And worse, her whole lower body was on display save for the panty thingy that was wrapped tightly in the middle of her vagina. The leggings she had on was as transparent as her light skin.

Her face was shinning with the ridiculously thick make up and bronzer she had all over. And she was wearing a bright red wig. Red wig!

Before I could stop my sharp tongue, I heard myself scream in horror at her appearance.

"What the heck are you wearing?!!"

CHAPTER TWO.

✶ Sansa*

I clamped my hand over my mouth the moment I heard my harsh voice fill the room.

I shouldn't have said that out loud.

"Oh, come on. We're in school for Christ's sake! That's where we get to do whatever we want to do." She replied me with a charming laugh.

I was a bit relieved that she wasn't offended by my outburst. I knew I would have been angry if it had been me.

Before I could say any other thing, she jumped into me with a tight hug. I yelped before trying to hug her back.

"OMG! You're so pretty! Look at your hair.. And my, oh, my.. Just look at that yansh!"

I thought I would choke at her words. This girl called Amarachi was going to be a handful. I gasped as I felt the hard smack on my ass. She just hit my ass!

"Chai! Your boyfriend is really lucky. I wish I had goods like you.. See boobs nau!" She was grinning from ear to ear as she kept looking me over.

"Um.. I don't have a boyfriend. And I don't even wish to have." I replied in a dead tone.

"See you, I give you 2 weeks. You'll be humping a guy soon." I knew she was joking, she was a sweet girl really, But I couldn't stop the feeling of angry that waved through me because of her words.

I was still easily prone to my panic attacks once someone started to talk about anything sexual. It was like I was allergic to it.

She continued on anyway. "I hope you don't mind my own boyfriend coming to see me here sha, he's a very active guy and we fuck each other at any chance—"

My head muted out the rest of her words as I felt my skin start to get clammy and irritable. That feeling was back. Like the room was too small, and some invisible hand was set to grab and fling me across the room....

I shut my eyes tight and took a deep breath, trying to wash down the terrible feeling. I couldn't let her know what was wrong with me.

"Excuse me! I have to pee." I said and rushed with blinding speed to the toilet. I heard the surprise in her voice as she asked if she had said anything wrong. I couldn't give an answer.

AFTER some minutes, I went back to the room and proceeded to make some conversation with her.

We got talking as soon as we started arranging the place. I told her I was studying business Administration while she was studying mass comm. English major. No wonder she talks like a parrot.

I found that I liked her, even though I had a problem with the way she dressed. She was a really friendly person and I knew we would get along.

"So... Are you working?" I asked her, minutes after we had settled down. She stopped clicking on her phone and raised her head up to look at me.

"Working what?" She asked with incredulity.

"Well... I just thought you would have applied for IT. You know.. That way you can earn money for yourself and get a better understanding of your course..."

I wasn't even done when I her sharp bark of laughter stopped me short. I hated when people laughed at me. I really hated it.

"Work! Why will I work abeg? My dad sends me monthly allowance that is even more than some graduate's salary. My boyfriend spends money on me like it's his job! So what do I possibly want to work for again?"

She chuckled, smiling mockingly at me.

"Well.. I just thought... Any way, I applied at an audit firm for the post of an assistant auditor." I said to her.

"Wow.... So you really want to work? Why...?"

"Well... Apart from the fact that I want to earn the little I can for myself, I just want to get a hang of.. what I'll be doing in the nearest future."

"So.. Is your dad aware of this?" She asked with a narrowed eyes.

"Yes. He even spoke to my supervisor." I lied. I couldn't tell her that my dad hardly knew anything about my school.

I had made Aliu talk to my IT supervisor in place of my dad, and I had easily intercepted my dad's mails when he wasn't around.

"Besides... Apart from exams period, I have classes just 3 times a week. I can't just stay at home all day doing nothing."

"Uh.. Madam.. I don't know.. You can FLEX YOUR LIFE??" I laughed at the way she exclaimed at the last statement. Amarachi was a very funny girl.

"So where will you be working?"

"Gentry Audit firm." I replied.

Amarachi gasped and sat up with an expression of astonishment on her face.

"Gentry? That's the Same name as our school!"

Oh. I hadn't even realized that.

"Yeah, that's true oh" I replied.

"I'm happy for you. From what I know.. The Gentrys are one of the biggest corporations in Nigeria. Working at one of their firms will earn you immediate connection."

I wasn't really concerned about the reputation of where I was working, I just wanted to work, but I smiled and moved in to lean into the hug she offered, inhaling her sweet perfume.

We talked some more before going to bed. I laid down with a long sigh of contentment and anticipation of my first lecture tomorrow.

CLASS WAS PRETTY MUCH BORING THE NEXT DAY. There was hardly any lectures, just lecturers introducing themselves and their products to us. I didn't have a problem with it because I was mostly on my my own.

Occasionally, some guys waved at me and some made small talk, but I didn't bother to mingle. I was determined not to make any real friends around here. Well.. Except for Amarachi.

I smiled as I remembered how she had woken me up earlier today with what she called her 'project breakfast in bed'.

She was a good cook. I would give her that. And we even ended up talking about other random things. I smiled even more widely as I remembered how I'd almost screamed at her outfit for the day.

The skirt had been so small and tight that she could barely put a foot out, her butt had been practically popping out of the tiny thing, and her transparent, white, bra-top.

I'd managed to convince her to change into something less revealing and surprisingly, she had agreed. Albeit, with a little persuasion.

"And so.. That is all for today. If you have any questions for me, you can see me in my office at the second floor of the management faculty. Block 003...."

Class was officially over. I didn't waste time in packing my books into my small backpack.

I was in the hallway when my phone rang. It was my supervisor calling. Geez!

"Good afternoon sir.. Mr Emeka." I greeted into the phone after a brief 'Hello'.

"Afternoon, Miss Osaze. I called you to inform you that there's free period for you to observe your facial interview this afternoon. The Auditor is around as we speak."

My head perked up in surprise and excitement. "Really??"

"Yes, Miss Osaze. Should I set the arrangement for your interview? Once you're done you can..."

"Yes! Yes sir! In fact.. I'm done with class. I can come over now sir. I'll take the public cab so I can be faster." I replied with open enthusiasm. I was so happy.

"Okay dear," He replied with a chuckle. Probably because of my excitement. "I'll make the arrangements."

I switched off my phone and began descending down the stairs with barely hidden excitement.

I was about to cross to the last block when I ran into someone. I caught myself immediately so I could look at the person before dropping a quick apology.

It was a guy in my class. He'd been looking at me in a creepy way when I'd first walked into the class. I felt my pulse start to race at the creepy way he looking at me, even now.

"H.. Hi" I muttered and moved to walk away. He followed me.

"HI.. You're in my class.. What's your name?" He asked, his voice so dark and thick that it literally made me shiver.

"Um.. Yes. Sansa." I replied in a tiny voice. Stop being scared Sansa. I silently scolded myself.

"Sansa? Wow... That's.. An unusual name." He replied with a slight chuckle. His face was so dark and he almost looked mean, Save for the consistent smile that was on his face.

"Thank you. I.. I have to go now. Bye."

The moment I took a step forward, I felt his hand snake through my left arm with a tight grip. I screamed and jumped as I slapped his hand as hard as I could.

"Let me go!!!"

His eyes widened in alarm and confusion as I stared back at him. My breaths were coming out frantically and fast.

"Woah.. I'm sorry, I..."

Before he could go on, I quickly ran away, covering my head in shame at my unnecessary outburst. I quickly dabbed at the tears that had formed in my eye the moment I got into the cab.

****

"Miss Osaze, you're early oh. I presume there was hardly any traffic." Mr Emeka said as he shook my hand. I didn't expect him to look this... Old.

He was wearing a funny, purple suit, or coat, that was a little too big for him. His face look strained and his white hair was very much visible.

How does he have a young man's voice?

I dismissed such wayward thoughts about the poor man and returned the greetings with a polite smile.

"Thank you so much, sir."

He directed me to where I was supposed to sit and wait. I was relieved when I met two other young girls, who like me, were waiting to have their interview.

After 20 minutes, I was still waiting. I kept wondering what was keeping the man from seeing me. I hated the fact that I was too excited to have my first interview.

I turned my head around and saw a small coffee Cafe at the other end of the reception. I think I need some.

I walked over to the Cafe and quickly ordered for a cup of coffee. Once I collected it, I turned— and unfortunately collided into someone.

I tried to gasp as the breath left my lungs with the force of my hit. The second time today!

"I.. I'm so sorry.."

I raised my head up to look at the person I had just ran into, and I automatically froze.

I gasped as I stared into his dark, dark eyes. Bottomless pits. His face looked like it was carved from stone. Not just any stone, a stone made of solid gold.

He was tall, so tall he hovered over me. My eyes moved to his full, pink lips. I couldn't think. I couldn't move. I just kept staring. He was like a god.. Or a runway model. How can someone be this handsome??!

I expected the panic attacks I always felt when I was around young guys like him to hit me, but it never came. I was too transfixed to even feel scared.

I felt my face flame up as his eyes also ran me up and down. I felt unbelievably shy and exposed.

I was however, not ready for his next, rude statement. Which angered me.

"Can't you watch where you're going, girl!"

He was glaring at me. I opened my mouth to answer.. Then closed it as I couldn't come up with any words.

Sansa what is happening to you?!

CHAPTER THREE

IT TOOK ME A FEW MOMENTS TO REGAIN MY mushed senses. As soon as his harsh words registered in my brain, I felt my face blaze up in anger. Who did he think he was? He just felt he could talk to strangers in a rude manner just because he had a fine face??!

I will show him what rude is!

"Excuse me, Who the hell do you think you are?! You're the one who should actually watch where you're going. You literally had your whole head buried in your phone!"

I saw his eyes widen in shock, like he didn't believe that I had just spoken back to him. I felt my limbs relax with satisfaction as I watched his handsome face scrunch up unattractively with barely leashed anger.

"Do you have any idea of who you're talking to?" He whispered in a dangerously low tone. His voice was calm but I could feel the waves of anger that emanated from him.

My body unconsciously stiffened with fear as I stared at his wide, angered face. No! I refuse to cower.

"Oh, Yes I have an idea. I'm talking to the president's son, right?.. Or no.. I think I'm talking to the prince of Egypt??.. Or, In fact, maybe I'm talking to a god right?!"

His mouth hung wide open in shock as if he still couldn't believe someone could talk to him in such manner. He must be used to people treating him like a god. I didn't care. I wouldn't accept being bullied by someone I don't know.

"You really need to watch what you say to strangers, little girl. Get out of my way."

Before I could process what was happening, I felt a hard jerk to my shoulder as he roughly shoved me aside and made his way forward.

What the hell?!

I was about to rush after him in the blurry haze of my anger when the mention of my name from the office where I was to be interviewed stopped me. It was my turn. I hesitantly turned around and went forward, momentarily glancing back to where the rude guy was retreating to. Jerk.

****

"SO HOW WAS your interview today?" Amarachi asked in a voice that barely hid her excitement and curiosity.

"Well.. I start tomorrow!" I screeched in equal excitement, and bursted into laughter as she jumped up with a loud scream from her lungs.

"OMG! I'm so happy for you! Student and worker.. That's one sexy combination o"

"I'll just be starting with the basics though. And my working hours is very minimum. And, although, I don't have any idea of what I'll be doing yet,

The manager gave me my own personal system!" I replied with a roll of my eyes.

"Wow, That is so wonderful!... I say we celebrate! Let's order 5 bottles of wine.. Or beer!"

Uh-oh. "Um.. Amarachi, I don't really drink..."

"Oh come on! You don't drink too? Nawa ooo, kukuma tell me you're a church evangelist na!" Amarachi whined with a accusatory glare at me.

I couldn't tell her that I had a strict rule of abstaining from alcohol. Few years ago, I'd taken to drinking. So much so that it became a bad habit to cure my depression and anger.

I remembered the last time I got drunk, I'd beaten up two of my friends at school and knocked down the teachers table. Even so, when I'd been reported to my father about my abusive behavior, the man hadn't even cared. He'd simply sent Aliu to come pick me up. Aliu was the one who helped me in stopping that habit. He'd taken me to a therapist, who had given me the steps to stop my addiction for drinking.

"I just don't enjoy the taste of it, seriously." I lied.

"Hmm, okay o. If you say so. How about we order pizza and some hollandia yogurt? Is that fine?" She asked in a hopeful tone.

I realized with a jolt that Amarachi wanted us to be friends. Real friends. I hadn't had any real friends asides Mr Aliu.

I smiled warmly at her, seeing her pretty face break into a smile also. "Okay!" I replied with a tentative clap of my palms.

As Amarachi began making the orders, I found my mind wandering off to the handsome face of the rude guy I had clashed with earlier today. I couldn't fathom why I still had him in my mind.

****

Richard (Pov)

THE STENCH of alcohol mixed with the strong smell of sweat and sex lingered in the air of the exclusive club, owned by my dad. One of the biggest club in the territory.

I glanced at my uncle, Mr David Gentry, who was comfortably seated with the tiny lady who was straddling him. My face turned to the chubby girl who was also enclosed in my own arms, with her almost naked body rubbing all over me.

She was smiling tentatively at me. It was all too clear that she was waiting for the go-ahead, just to please me. Ladies always wanted to please me. It came with the name. A Gentry. The name alone made ladies to always treat me like a god.

My mind unconsciously went back to the little brat I had ran into at the cafeteria.

Maybe I'm talking to a god right?

Those words kept repeating in my head, making me scowl in anger and amazement. That girl had spoken to me rudely, with such annoyingly taunting sarcasm that I had felt like strangling her, right then and there. But I've never had that toxic trait of putting my hands upon women. So I had let her talk to me as she pleased.

"Baby..." I was broken from my reverie by the seductive voice of the girl in front of me, she was staring at my lips expectantly. "Do you want a blow job? I'm pretty good..."

I tensed as I felt her fingers sneak neatly into my slacks as she tried to grab my erection. My hands shot out to stop her from continuing.

"No.. No.. I.." I gently pushed her off my legs and sat up straight. "I'm not interested. Not in the mood. Sorry."

The girl's face fell with disappointment and she moved to walk away.

"Wait." I said, making her stop to turn back with a hopeful smile.

I reached into my pocket and pulled out several thousand naira notes, and handed it to her. She stared at my hand in shock.

"Here. Take this and take the night off." I told her before turning towards my uncle.

The girl murmured her thanks with shyness, making me chuckle with amusement at how shy she was acting now, considering how she'd been sitting comfortably on me a while ago.

I waved a dismissive hand at her and turned to my Uncle, who had a funny look on his face.

"Hey, Uncle. I'll be heading home now."

"Why? What's wrong?"

"Nothing. I'm just stressed. I have a long day tomorrow also. I'll be heading out now." I said as I got up and left the room dark room.

Outside, my Car, a black tinted Lamborghini was parked with three girls taking selfies in front of it.

Women. I thought with a chuckle. They'd probably post the picture on social media, indicating that they owned the car, when In fact, they didn't even know the owner.

Their heads turned towards me as they heard my footsteps. I sighed in exhaustion as I saw their faces lit up as I walked closer.

They were openly whispering now. About me.

"Excuse me, ladies." I said, waiting for them to move out of the way.

"HI! Sorry, we were just taking pictures." One of the girls whispered in a cheerful tone.

"Alright. Can you move away now?" I asked Impatiently.

"Not until you give me your mobile number, so we can all snap pictures in front of your car next time." The girl said. She looked like she was the leader of their dumb girly group.

I smirked at her. "OK. Don't move away. Maybe you don't value your legs."

I entered my car and turned on the engine without hesitation. I smiled in satisfaction as the girls hurriedly moved away, screaming.

As I drove home, I kept wondering if the rude girl would have stepped out of the way when I started my car. Probably not.

I recalled how she'd stared at me with an expression of.. Awe, as she looked at my face. I recalled how her lips had looked so soft and supple, and how her big doe eyes had gazed at me in wonder, her beautiful darkened cheeks.....

Stop thinking about her! She's not worth it!

****

"Good morning Richard, I sent some files to your mail last night,.. I'm guessing you didn't check it?" My uncle announced the moment I stepped into my office.

"Good morning, Uncle. And no, I didn't check my mails. Any problem?"

"Uh.. No. I sent the info about the student who will be working closely with you. She's supposed to have arrived an hour ago...."

The errant knock on the glass door stopped our conversation. Uncle David swiftly opened the door to let the person in.

I raised my head at the person and suffered an unanticipated shock immediately I recognized her.

"Hi! Good morning. I.. I'm.. So sorry for arriving late. The rain.. Traffic.. I..." Her anxious voice trailed off as her eyes landed on me.

"You!" She yelled at me with a red, angry face.

"Oh, you have met each other?" Uncle David asked in a confused tone, his eyes darting back and forth between us.

"Oh Yes, Uncle. We certainly have met each other." I said with a satisfactory gleam, watching as her eyes widened with fear while I got up and started stalking towards her with slow, predatory steps. I took in her drenched form and noted that she was wet all over.

"You see, Uncle," I continued with a smirk "We met Yesterday, when her mouth was running like tap water." I said, and had the satisfaction to watch her gasp outrageously. Good.

"Today, it turns out that she's going to be working for me. Right, Miss..?"

"Well.. She technically doesn't know you." Uncle David said to me. Clearly oblivious. "So.. Sansa, this is Richard Gentry. He's a final year student in the Gentry University, owned by his father, And this is his first accounting firm and he's a co-owner of the place ."

She didn't give any reply. I watched as she gulped and swallowed. Trying to come up with something. Nothing came out. I was beginning to enjoy this too much.

"Um... Well.. I better leave you to sort things out with her. Take care, Miss Osaze." He said and walked out. Leaving her alone with me.

****

Sansa

HOW IS THIS POSSIBLE?! I thought, as I stared into the face of my nightmare. He was my boss??

"Um..." I started with a gulp. "I'm sorry I came in so late.. I.. I was delayed because of the rain, there was hardly any transport and..."

"I didn't ask for an explanation, Madam. Will you shut up for a minute?" He interrupted me with a frown on his face.

I needed to control the anger I was feeling. Getting angry at someone above me would cause problems for me. It was what caused the embarrassment I was currently trying to hide.

"Well.. My name is Sansa Osaze, I..."

"Sansa Osaze?" He raised an eyebrow.

"Yes..."

"Not only have you arrived late on your first day at work, you arrived looking like a wet rat!"

"I just explained my ordeal! I was beaten by the rain—"

"I don't care about your ordeal! Go home."

I stared at him in shock. I had known that today would be a tough day for me since I set my eyes on him, but I hadn't expected him to fire me on the spot. Was he actually serious??

"I will not go home! You have no right to send me away just because my dress is wet." I replied him in a defiant voice.

"I'm giving you half an hour to go home and change your appearance. If not, kiss your job goodbye, you brat!" He roared in my face.

"What?! I can't go home! It's far!" I cried.

"Your time is ticking, off you go now." He said dismissively as he started to move backwards.

Maybe I could try to persuade him.

"Please, I can't go back home at this hour. It would—"

"Get out!" He boomed furiously.

I felt the back of my eyelids burn with unshed tears, But I raised my chin up and glared back at him. I wouldn't let him see me weak. Never.

"Alright. I'll be back soon, Mr Gentry."

I opened the door and stepped out. I went ahead and boarded a quick cab to the hostel. On the way, I kept thinking of how I'd cope with Richard Gentry.

That guy was going to make my life a living hell.

****

CHAPTER FOUR

✱ Sansa*

I sent another additional 200k to your funds. Make sure you put it to good use.   *Your Dad.*

I reread the text that I'd just received into my mail about an hour ago, which was from my father.

I was in the safe confines of my new, tiny office but it still felt like I was exposed. My skin suddenly felt clammy and I could practically feel the walls closing in on me.

It was as if a fierce battle was going on under my sweaty skin, trying to pull me into that state of depression I never wanted to be in.

This always happened every time I thought of my father, trying to forgive him, but knowing it probably would never happen.

He killed mom.

Three words that always taunted me relentlessly anytime I tried to forgive him.

I swiftly pulled my system open and clicked on the button to reply.

Sansa to Collins O. Osaze

Thank you. But I have enough cash with me. Will send it back to your secretary. S. O

Not waiting for a reply, I closed the laptop with a loud snap before burying my head into my arms and finally succumbing to my raging feelings as I burst into low, nerve-wracking sobs.

I didn't know how long I stayed in that position until I was broken out of my trance, startled when I heard the sound of my door flicking open. I knew without a doubt that it was Richard Gentry.

I wasn't able to clean my eyes as quickly as I would have wished to, when my eyes clashed with his. Silence. We stared at each other, him standing frozen in front of the office door, me sitting behind the desk like a wood log behind the desk.

After some moments, I cleared my throat to break the unnerving silence. "Um.. Uh... Is.. Is there something you need?"

He just kept staring at me, his dark eyes glaring holes into my shrinking body. I hated that I was feeling conscious of him, like he was warming his way up my skin. I hated this feeling.

"Why are you here?" I asked again, in a firmer, strict tone. I glared back at him.

"I would ask you why your whole face is soaked with tears, but I don't care." He stated with a scowl at me. "I wanted to ask if you have a good idea of how to type and print out the weekly financial reports."

"Oh, yeah. Mrs Temi gave me the instructions." I replied.

Mrs Temi was Richard's secretary and righthand-woman. When we'd spoken, and I'd told her about the way he'd treated me badly on the first day of my IT, she'd simply smiled at me, explaining that he was not a bad man, he had just wanted to test me.

I'd smiled and nodded but hadn't believed her one bit. Richard Gentry was a wicked human being and I disliked him with a shocking intensity.

"Alright." He replied, then glanced at his wristwatch. "It's 11am, you can take a 30 minute break, but be back early and stick to the little work you've been given."

And he was out the door. I sighed as I got up from my seat, pulling my small Gucci bag-purse along with me. I could use some snacks. I was pretty much hungry anyway.

I got out and made my way to the elevator which would take me downstairs, where the cafeteria was located. Where I mistakenly met the jerk.

When I got to the cafeteria, I was pleasantly surprised to see few people there. I quickly moved to the front desk and proceeded to order my lunch.

As soon as the waiting guy received my order, I moved on to climb onto the high stool so I could wait for my lunch.

I hadn't realized my purse had fallen off until I saw someone's head close to the ground. He was picking up my purse. A thief!

"Hey! My purse!" I yelled as he got hold of the purse.

"Relax, your purse fell off your arm just now and I just wanted to pick it up for you." The guy replied, raising his head up with a tight-lipped smile at me.

I felt my face flush in embarrassment. I should have known that he wasn't a robber with the way he was elegantly dressed.

"Oh.. I'm so sorry, I didn't mean to..."

"It's fine. I won't take any offense if you let me buy you lunch." The guy replied. I got a good look at his face and I realized he was much older than me. Maybe five or six years older. I was probably talking to a senior.

"Oh.. No.. Um.. Thank you, but I—"

"Oh come on, it's fine. Really. My name is Ayo and I work here. Nice to meet you."

I accept his stretched hand and shook him lightly before withdrawing my hand. I eyed him skeptically as I smiled back at him. He looked to be a nice kind of guy. But I wouldn't be too sure.

"Hi.. I'm Sansa." I replied in a small voice.

"Beautiful name. I'm guessing you just started working here?"

"Yes. Assistant Auditor." I replied cheerfully.

"Woah, that's impressive. You're done with school?"

"No. In fact, I'm a fresher."

"Oh? So that means you applied for IT?" He asked, raising his dark eyebrow as if he was surprised.

"Yeah. I really like it here and my job is very easy. So.. What do you do?" I asked him. I found my self relaxing into the harmless conversation even as I collected my food and went to sit on the dining.

He told me he had just finished serving last year and that he started working here the last week as the human resources manager. He was apparently 27 years old, but he didn't look it.

After some time, I looked down at my wristwatch and realized that I would be running late to finish my task.

"I have to go back to work now, Ayo. Thank you for buying my lunch, I really appreciate it." I said, standing up to drop the tray of finished food on the counter.

"It's nothing, Sansa. I could escort you to your office?.. If you don't mind?" He added immediately he saw my worried expression. I didn't want him to feel bad, so I accepted.

"Um.. Sure." I said.

He broke into a wide grin and ushered me out of the Cafe.

"So, Sansa.." Ayo said with a stop at my office door. "It's been nice talking to you. Maybe I can come check on you some other time?"

"Yes, Sure. Thanks, Ayo." I replied brightly. He looked like he wanted to give me a hug, but he didn't because of how quickly I moved back. I didn't want any close contact with any male. That would be breaking my rule.

We said our byes and I entered my office, smiling as I looked down at my purse.

"What were you doing with him?"

I screamed the moment I heard the dark, angry voice boom from inside my office. I stared at Richard. He was sitting slightly on my desk, glaring indignantly at me.

"How did you get in here!" I yelled at him. I didn't care if my voice was very loud. I was too angry to even care. I was livid.

He smirked at me and began walking slowly towards me, wide shoulders rippling with commanding force as he took each slow steps towards me. My heart was beating loudly now, every part me screaming out in alarm.

He stopped in front of me, effectively blocking me out from the rest of the room. All I could see was him. He was so tall.

"The innocent peanut that started work here just yesterday, is already flirting her ass about the building!" He exclaimed angrily.

I gasped in outrage and balled my fists out of anger. Was he really serious? He was tracking me?

"What are you even saying??" I asked hoarsely. I was feeling so conscious of his closeness to me and angry at what he was saying about me. The feelings were muddling up my senses, making me confused and afraid.

"The CCTV camera showed how you were practically sucking off the thumbs of one of our new workers! Have you no shame?!"

"What—No offense, Mr Richard but I can see you're clearly not in your senses! I have other things to do, please get out." I said and tried to move out of his blockage.

"Come back here! I'm not done talking to you!"

I gasped as he instantly pulled on my arm and dragged me into his wide chest. I felt all the breath I had left whoosh out of my lungs as I collided with his strong, hard body.

I stood frozen. I couldn't move. It was like time all together had stopped as we stared into each other's eyes, drowning. I gulped as I saw his eyes move downwards to my lips. Was he going to kiss me? No...

But I couldn't react. It was like my body was being controlled, like I didn't own any of the muscles and bones because everything felt mushy. He was so close. Impossibly close. I can't allow this.

I held my breath as his head began sloping downwards. He was going to kiss me!

I stared at him with my eyes widened, frantic, but I couldn't do anything.

Then, miraculously, the spell was broken as the door opened once again.

"Hello, Sansa. I wanted to inform..."

We speedily broke apart as Mr David, Richard's uncle stared at us in surprise. He must have seen that we were holding each other. Chai!

"Um.. Am I disturbing something?...."

"No!— No, sir. Mr... Richard was just leaving." I turned and glared at Richard, silently daring him. He was also glaring at me and his uncle. I just wanted him to get out. He was causing too much problems to my mental health and sanity. In such a short time.

Fortunately, Richard took the cue and left.

"Is Richard giving you a hard time? Did he attack you?" Mr David asked once Richard was out of the room.

"No, Sir. He's not. I'm sorry..."

"It's Alright. Just... Be careful. Richard... He's a tough guy. Okay?"

I smiled at his caring words. "Okay, Sir."

"Alright. I'll leave you to yourself now. Have a nice day tomorrow at school." He said.   "Thanks, sir." I replied and waited till he left before I slumped into my seat with my heart practically hammering out my chest.

****

Harder Bobby! Give it to me! Yes! Arrgh!

My eyebrows furrowed as I got closer to my hostel room. I had just left the firm some minutes ago and was back home.

"What's making Amarachi shout like a mad woman like this??" I asked my self as I got closer.

I reluctantly opened the door, and screamed at the horrible scene that played in front of me.

Amarchi was naked on top of a guy that was naked. They were having sex vigorously. I screamed in horror.

"AMARACHI ARE YOU MAD??!! WHAT IS THIS!!"

Amarachi fell off the guy with a loud shriek as she looked at me with palpable shock.

"San.. Sansa.. You.. I'm sorry.."

"Did you plan a threesome for me, chi-chi? This babe's hot sha" The stupid, horrible looking guy whispered lazily as he used the blanket that was my blanket, to cover his ugly member.

"That's it! I'm done. I can't be your roommate anymore!" I screamed at her in frustration.

"Sansa, I'm sorry!" She pleaded without even bothering to cover her naked body.

"Sorry for yourself! I'm moving out abeg!" I yelled at her before marching to the closet to remove my things.

I couldn't stay with someone who made me so uncomfortable with her sexual abilities. That was my own disability and I wasn't going to let her rub it in my face.

CHAPTER FIVE.

✱ Sansa*

"SANSA, I'M SORRY! PLEASE!" Amarachi pleaded even as I carried my heavy luggage and stopped at the entrance of our tiny hostel.

"You don't respect me, Amarachi. Because if you do, you won't bring your boyfriend here for sex, especially on my OWN BED! What happened to your own bed?!"

"Well.. He said.. Your mattress is stronger than mine.. So he'll be able to pound me very—"

"Shut up! I don't want to hear again!" I exclaimed as my face reddened in anger and frustration.

"Please.. Don't leave me." Amarachi urged with tears gathering around her eyes. "I never thought that you'll have a problem with me bringing my boyfriend here.. I promise it won't ever happen again!"

I backed myself out of her reach as she tried to embrace me. I could still vividly picture the horrible image of her on top of her boyfriend in my mind. I couldn't forgive her. Even though I was really tempted to.

"Give me any punishment you want, Sansa. But don't leave, please. If... If it makes you feel better, I'll leave instead."

"Where will you go to?" I asked. Worry lacing the anger in my tone.

"I'll... Just stay at an hotel nearby..."

I sighed as the guilt began to swim in. I didn't want her sleeping outside just because I was very mad at her. If something went wrong, I would be held responsible.

She had started to stroll into the closet when I stopped her.

"Don't worry. I'll stay." I derided between clenched teeth. I was too angry to even look at her, or the stupid guy that was seated so comfortably on our sofa.

Amarachi turned to me, her dark eyes gleamed with relief as she broke into a smile and moved in to hug me.

"But I haven't forgiven you! So just stay on your own abeg."

"Okay. Okay." Amarachi replied then turned to her boyfriend with a glare. "You, it's time to go. You're the one who got me into this mess with your insatiable libido!"

I hurriedly walked into the closet and closed the door with a loud bang. I didn't want to hear them talking about their sexual activities.

****

"One of the biggest concepts of Administration is the variety of responsibilities depending on the organization that they're employed with. Business activities are....."

I knew I was supposed to be listening to the nice lecture that was going on by the newly introduced lecturer, but my mind uncontrollably trailed off as thoughts of Richard Gentry went through my head.

I cringed as I thought about our last encounter, when he had almost kissed me. How was it possible that I was so attracted to him?

Yes, there was no doubt that he was an Adonis. all male perfection. And maybe it was my inexperience of being in the presence of guys like him, but it unsettled me. A lot. I was almost too scared of looking at him in the face and talking to him again.

What if he tried to kiss me again? What then would I do? Would I be able stop him? I couldn't afford to—

"Aren't you listening to me, Miss?"

I snapped out of my thoughts the moment I realized that the lecturer was pointing at me. He was asking me a question!

"Um.. Yes. Yes I'm listening." I replied with a frantic nod, glancing at him warily. He had that stern look on his face.

"Your body is in class, yet your mind and soul is probably with your boyfriend!" The man said angrily.

The whole class broke into laughter and giggles. I turned around slightly, and wished I didn't. They were all laughing at me.

Richard caused this! If I hadn't just been thinking of the jerk!

"I'm sorry, Sir..." I whispered in embarrassment. I felt like crying but I forced my self not to.

"Answer the question I asked you, Miss...?" The lecturer said, raising his eyebrows, as if to dare me not to answer.

"Um.. What.. What.. Could you repeat the question sir?" I asked and flinched as the class broke into another feats of laughter. They're all mad, I said to my self in annoyance.

The lecturer scowled at me and motioned for me to stand up. I stood up quickly and ended up knocking down my notebooks and pen. Oh God!

"I asked What the universal functions of Administration are. I listed them a while ago, so I see no reason why you shouldn't be able to give me at least two functions." He finished, still glaring at me.

I visibly swallowed as I glanced every which way. Unfortunately, I hadn't been listening and now I couldn't come up with a single word. The whole class was going to mock me to death.

"Say 'staffing and directing,' Sansa." It was a whisper behind me. I quickly glanced at the person and my eyes landed on the guy I had ran into the other day. The one who had tried to grab my arm.

He smiled apologetically at me. I knew he remembered how I'd reacted. I turned away from him and back to the lecturer, who was clearly angry now.

"WELL?!" His voice was raised a notch higher.

"Staffing and directing, Sir." I replied.

"Good." He said, then added as an after thought. "See me in my office after this class. The last floor beside the female toilet."

I nodded with a gulp before sitting down. I was surprised when I opened my book and found a tiny paper resting on it.

I'm sorry for the other time.

I smiled as I read the one sentence. I glanced back at him, he was looking much less intimidating unlike the last time. I waved at him and mouthed a 'thank you'.

MY NERVES WERE ALL OVER THE PLACE as I approached the lecturer's office an hour later. I really hoped I wasn't in trouble. God please.

"Come in," Came the answer after I knocked once.

I stepped into the office. It was a bit too dark considering it was still very bright outside.

"Hi, Sir. I'm so sorry about the other time in class, I'm not feeling fine so it—"

"I didn't ask for an explanation, dear." He interrupted my explanation with a sly smile. I frowned slightly at him.

"Oh? So.. Why did you ask me to.."

"I want to know more about you. What is your name?" He asked with that smile still on his face.

"Um.. My name is Sansa Osaze." I replied. I didn't like the way he was looking at me. Did he really just call me here to ask of my name??

"Sansa. I like you. You're a pretty girl." He stated.

At this point I already knew that he was hitting on me. I tried to hide my anger with much effort.

"I have a class to attend. I'll be leaving now." I gritted.

His eyes met the anger in my eyes. His smile grew, he was taunting me.

"Look.. Sansa. If you wish to do well this semester, it will be better if you listen to me. I'm just a nice guy who wants to take care of you. I don't bite.. Much. But if you don't... Well, it's up to you, and your grades, my dear."

His eyes trailed slowly all over my body in a way that made me feel like I was naked. I shivered as the fear settled deep inside me. A lecturer was hitting on me. Why Me of all people? I was so angry and scared, I felt the tears threaten to spill over my hot face.

His eyes settled on my barely exposed cleavage and I quickly moved to place my arms over my chest. He chuckled as I realized my actions.

"You can't blame me for looking, Sansa. God took his time to create you. Those hips are calling on to me like..."

"Enough!" I shouted at him. "You are very stupid, Sir! What kind of devilish attitude is that?! Hitting on a young girl. Aren't you shameless?!"

His whole demeanor instantly changed the moment those words left my mouth.

"You don't know who you're talking to, Sansa. One wrong move and you might find yourself thrown out of this school. We don't want that to happen now, do we?" He smirked. He knew he had the power to blackmail me and he was using it.

My hands were vibrating as I dug into my bag and fished out my phone. I went straight to my phone's gallery and clicked on the picture of the boy who put me in this situation in the first place.

It was kind of ironic that I hated Richard Gentry, yet I had his picture saved on my phone. I had scrolled through his pictures on his Instagram page the previous night, out of boredom, Or maybe curiosity. This particular picture had caught my attention because he looked so peaceful and... Sweet.

Unable to talk myself out of it, I had saved it on my phone. Now, I was unbelievably glad I did.

I turned the phone to show him the picture with a smirk.

"Who is this?" I asked him in a slight whisper, but with a firm tone.

His eyes widened the instant he saw the picture. Thank God.

"What do you know about Richard Gentry? He doesn't even know you!" The man retorted, his face widening with panic.

"Let me tell you something, if you do not know. Richard is my boyfriend.. And I work with him, at the Gentrys Accounting firm. All I have to do, is report you to him, I will give him the location of your office and your course number.... And then, you've lost your job. Just like that." I knew I wasn't supposed to lie about who Richard was to me, but I had to do it.

His face look flushed and Flustered. It was my turn to smirk at him.

"What! You.. You can't even.."

"Try me, Mr lecturer. And see how fast you're out of this university. In fact.. I know I'm not the first to fall into your trap. I will tell him about how you've been pestering young girls in the name of 'good grades!' I will even add salt and pepper to the story.. "

"Ah! Please.. Please, my dear. Don't do that now, I just wanted to give you advice on—"

"I don't need your advice! You're such a despicable man and I will make sure you regret hitting on me. You messed with the wrong one."

His eyes widened even more as he realized how much of a mistake he had made. It was almost too funny.

"Please.. We can talk this out." The lecturer said as he began to kneel down behind his desk. I couldn't help it, I bursted into laughter.

After I got enough control over my laughter, I smiled at him. "I will pity your life, and I'll act as if this never happened. But don't you ever try this with me, Or with any other girl. Never. Good day!"

I walked out of his office with my head held up high. I was damn proud of how I handled him with so much courage.

****

Richard

I gently pulled her into my arms, letting her straddle me as her soft hair cascaded around my face. That face so full of innocence and sweetness.

"Sansa...." I whispered as she spread her tiny fingers over my bare chest. I didn't know where we were, I didn't know how we got into this situation, but I would never trade it for anything in the world.

"Richard...." She whispered back, her lips moving lightly over my neck. I was straining for her touch. She was like a drug for me. I groaned as she grinded further into me, making me too hard for my trousers to be comfortable. This girl was going to finish me.

"Oh...."

Our bodies were wrapped into each other, there was barely any space to breathe. Her head came down to mine as our lips crashed in a earth shattering kiss.

"Boss?"

"Boss?"

My eyes snapped open. I glanced at the male in front of me, blinking severally as I tried to see the face of the person in front of me.

It was one of my servant, my house assistant. Apparently, I had fallen asleep on my couch after I'd drank too much earlier. I glanced down and saw the visible bulge that was outlined under my trouser. I'd been dreaming. About that annoying girl.

What the fuck!

"What's the issue, James?" I asked impatiently and quickly put the chair pillow over my groin to hide my erection.

"Your father is on the phone, Sir. He wants to speak with you. Said it's very important."

I collected the phone and raised it to my ear.

"Hi, Dad," I said.

"Richard, make preparations for the day after tomorrow at our hotel, my business partner will be arriving in Abuja tomorrow." My Dad said over the phone. No greetings.

"Okay. Preparations will begin. I'll notify the hotel manager." I replied in a tired voice.

"And.. His daughter will be coming along with him. So... I expect you to attend." He finished.

I scowled at the phone. "What do I have to do with your business partner's daughter? I won't attend, father." I spoke up without hesitation.

"You will have to attend, Richard. I want you and Folake to be date each other. It will help the merging of businesses move faster." My father snapped.

I sighed. I couldn't count how many lifeless dolls I had dated over the years in the name of business partnership.

"Alright, Father. Good night. Greet mom for me." I stated and didn't bother to wait before cutting the call.

My father was a manipulative man and he would get me to do whatever he wanted.

****

"Damn! You're one crazy girl, Sansa! How can you confidently pull a stunt like that with RICHARD GENTRY! What if he finds out??" Amarachi exclaimed after I told her about my day and the lecturer. I had finally forgiven her after she promised never to do something like that again.

I giggled at her shocked expression. "He won't find out jare, and if he does..."

The screeching of my phone stopped me from going on with our discussion. I glanced at the number. Unknown.

"Hello?"

"Sansa. It's Richard Gentry. Where are you at presently?" His voice boomed from the other side of the phone.

I instantly scooted out of my bed as soon as I heard his voice. Amarachi's eyes trailed after me with surprise and curiosity.

"Hi, Richard..." I started.

"Where are you? Answer me." He snapped impatiently.

"I'm at home. In my school hostel. Why?" I glanced at the wall clock. It was 7:45PM in the night. What could he be calling me for??

I froze with trepidation. What if Amarachi was right and the lecturer had told on me? I'm in trouble!

"Come out. I'm outside your hostel. I'm in a black Maserati." He quipped quickly.

"What? I.. It's late. You can't be allowed in the compounds around this time!" I exclaimed as I moved to the window. I gasped when I saw the shiny black car at parked beside the eatery area. He wasn't joking!

"I practically own the school, honey. I can come here anytime I want. Now, stop wasting my time and come out. It's urgent." Richard replied. I could almost picture him smirking in that arrogant way.

"But... But..." I was stuttering.

"If you quit shouting But... But.. And get dressed, you would have gotten here by now, stop wasting my time, girl."

"I can't come out. This is not my working hour. Please leave." I retorted angrily. My face flaming with heat.

"I will come in there, mind you, I know your exact room number, and pick you up, or you can just come down peacefully like a matured, sensible adult."

I sighed and retreated to get my working bag.

"I have to go, Amarachi. I'll be back soon." I said.

"Have fun. But not too much fun oo!" She called after me.

There would be no fun, I thought. I might just end up strangling Richard Gentry to death.

CHAPTER SIX

✱ Sansa*

HE WAS IGNORING ME. I couldn't fathom why he kept ignoring me on a daily basis, for the past two weeks, or why I was even bothered about him ignoring me in the first place.

I just felt like I needed to figure him out. To know what was wrong. Today he's hot, tomorrow he would be cold. It was almost like he had very serious bipolar issues.

My mind flashed back to that night when he had come to pick me up at my hostel. He'd taken me back to the office where we'd worked for almost 2 hours.

We'd made small conversation and even laughed a bit. I'd felt like we were making progress with each other, until I'd picked a call from Ayomide, who called to inform me that he wouldn't be coming to work the next day.

After the short call, he hardly spoke to me, only when he needed to give me an order.

"Something on your mind?"

I looked up at Ayomide, who was still sipping the beverage like it had some magic to it.

We were both eating at the cafeteria, on our lunch break. It had become more of an habit since we met each other. Ayomide was a very nice and jovial guy and I liked how respectful he was.

"Um... No.. Nothing jare, I'm just thinking of my project assignment in school." I stated, not quite meeting his probing eyes.

"I'm sure you'll do well. You are a very brilliant lady." He had something close to adoration in his eyes as he continued to gaze at me. I smiled back at him appreciatively. He was always optimistic and supportive.

"Thank you, Ayo. By the way.. I like your current haircut. Seems you don't joke with your hairstyles cause it's always topnotch." I teased. Ayo was what you would call an attractive nerd.

He had this slim figure that drew innocent girls to him, and I knew for a fact that he had girls on queue for him. He was also very appealing but he didn't have that Intimidating look like....

"Well... I like to take care of my self, yunno?" He replied with a casual, self assured smile.

"Goooood" I drawled with a playful giggle.

"So.. I've been meaning to tell you something, Sansa,"

"Oh? What's wrong?" I asked with curiosity.

"Well... I like you, Sansa. Not just any normal like, I think I have feelings for you. You're this sweet, wonderful girl that any guy would be lucky to have,"

I gulped as his words registered in my head. Ayo had feelings for me. How would I handle this?

"You don't have to say anything, Sansa" He continued, "I just wanted to let it out. Just so you know."

"Ayo... I like you too, but just as a dear friend. I'm not interested in a relationship right now, I just want to focus on my academics." I finished.

"I'm sorry..." I added, as I noticed his gaze drop with disappointment.

"Oh, come on! It's fine. I'll always be here for you, though."

I was so glad that he was able to laugh it off. He was a good friend to me and I didn't want to loose him.

"Thank you, Ayo."

LATER THAT DAY, When I was preparing to leave the office, I decided to check on Richard, just to satisfy my curiosity.

I knocked silently on the door before opening.

"Oh, hi!" A lady quipped from behind the table.

Richard wasn't around. Where is he? And who is this women sitting here like she owns the place??

"Um.. Hi... I came to see Richard Gentry..."

"Oh, I'm sorry dear, he's not around. He hasn't really been around this week. I'm just here overseeing things for him." She explained.

But that's supposed to be my work! I thought furiously.

"I'm Folake." She stated. "I'm a.... Friend and business partner of his."

"Oh, Alright, Ma'am. Sorry for the disturbance. I'll be leaving now." I said and went to turn back, but she stopped me.

"What's your name? I can inform him of your visit." she replied, smiling cheerfully at me.

"Um.. Sansa."

"Oh, what an intriguing name. Maybe we can talk sometime?" She asked with a hopeful lift of her perfectly drawn eyebrows.

"Sure. Bye!" I replied with a smile before exiting the room.

I kept wondering who she was. What did she and Richard have together? That's not my business sha.

****

I glanced around at the even newer faces I was seeing today at the school eatery. New students were arriving at the hostel and the faculties.

There was a particular girl that had arrived a few days ago, she was rumored to be one of the local government chairman's daughter.

Unknowingly, I had clumsily stepped on her foot one time when we were queueing for our badges, and she had taken offense and warned me never to cross her path again, Even though I'd apologized countless times.

"So, where will you do your project experiments?" I asked Jamal, who was stuffing his face with burger and creamy salad. I almost laughed out loud at how funny he looked.

Since the time he'd rescued me in class and dropped the letter saying he was sorry, I'd taken a liking to him. Now we were close friends. He was a very brilliant boy.

"My Aunt's place. She has this big chart at home, and I can use it anytime I wish. What about you?" He asked, his voice muffled by the junk that was filled in his mouth. I shook my head slowly at him.

"I think I'll probably ask my roommate, Amarachi, to borrow me hers. She has a similar project and bought the chart a long time ago. But if it doesn't work with my calculations, then you must be ready to welcome me to your aunt's place."

"Ooooh! She's finally coming over!" He pumped his dark fists in the air as a sign of celebration.

"Shut up," I replied with a giggle while shaking my head back and forth.

"Sansa....look who's at your back." Jamal whispered with a mischievous smile.

I reluctantly turned backwards and almost bursted into laughter when I saw the shameless lecturer, Mr Gabriel. He was sitting all by himself at a corner while operating on his device.

"I swear ehn, If I'd been told that Mr Gabriel would come to the eatery without a single student on his arm, I wouldn't have believed it! Omo! Na you oh!"

I laughed lightly at his appraisal. It was true. Since I'd had the clash with him, news had flied around about Mr Gabriel being a 'born again'.

The only people that knew what truly happened were Amarachi and Jamal. The pawn in the game wasn't even aware, and I would rather keep it that way. I knew there would be trouble for me if Richard found out and I didn't want that to happen.

But it did.

I knew there was something wrong when everywhere became deathly silent, save for the silent, curious whispers I could distinctly hear.

My ear caught one. "So he finally has a girlfriend?!"

I glanced at the ladies who were whispering to themselves. I noticed their attention was on someone who stood at the food counter. I turned to check out who they were thoroughly inspecting.

My heart broke into a halt the moment my eyes landed on him. I flinched with shock and surprise as I saw him hold on to a lady who was facing the other side....

My mind raced with fear as every eyes focused on them. Then the lady turned. I almost reeled back in perpetual shock. The lady at his office! Folake!

My body began to tremble as they moved forward, coming towards our way. My eyes skated through them with jealousy. This was not happening.

"Sansa. I think we should leave now." Jamal stated silently. But I was too immobile to give a reply.

Then I watched in horror as Richard and Folake stopped in front of the lecturer as they greeted each other.

He will tell Richard!

"SANSA. LET'S LEAVE NOW." Jamal whispered again, this time he took a hold of my arm.

"How is the business going, Richard?" I heard The lecturer ask.

"Fine, thank you, Mr Gabriel." Richard replied in a deep tone.

A moment before the lecturer spilled the words, his gaze glanced my way with a mocking smile.

"Did you come here to see your girlfriend, Sansa Osaze? She's over there." He said loudly, for everyone to hear. And the gasps that filled the room confirmed that every one heard.

I was in deep shit.

****

Richard

I paused abruptly at the sound of her name. Did he just say girlfriend?

My gaze flew over to where she stood. She almost looked like a statue, save for the color on her rosy cheeks.

I was so shocked and confused that I couldn't utter a word immediately. I knew lecturer Gabriel. He was a rat and a hopeless womanizer.

What the hell made him think Sansa Osaze was my girlfriend??

"What do you mean.. Girlfriend?" I asked slowly, staring back and forth at Sansa and Gabriel.

"She claimed she's your girlfriend, and everyone here is aware of it. I thought you would be aware of it?" Mr Gabriel replied with a smile and pointed at Sansa.

"What? I do not know her." I pulled Folake closer to me. "This is my girlfriend."

The whole room broke into series of howls and gasps. I looked and Sansa and saw that she was crying already. Good. I wouldn't accept her lying about me. After flirting with that stupid coworker all week.

I instantly realized what was happening. I knew why she had lied about me being her boyfriend.

She actually lied about him being her boyfriend! What a bitch! She's shameless!

I greeted my teeth in anger as I heard the whispers flowing around. Sansa was being bullied. I had no idea why that bothered me a lot.

I heard her hurried footsteps as she ran out of the hall in tears, with a small annoying boy, who I guessed was her close friend, running after her.

"I want to see you in private, Mr Gabriel." I stated with a glare at him.

"I HAVE NO IDEA WHAT HAPPENED JUST NOW, MR GABRIEL, BUT I WANT TO GIVE YOU A FAIR WARNING" I stared at the lecturer with disgust. I knew without a doubt what he was up to no good with my Sansa.

"If you ever go close to Sansa Osaze again, or you ever try to bother her even the tiniest bit, you will not only lose your job, but I will make sure you lose your life!!...understood?" I murmured, smiling with satisfaction as I saw his eyes widen with fright.

"Ye... Yes.. Sir." He stammered.

I patted him lightly at the back, before walking out the door with a loud bang of the door.

****

My head was aching so bad. I'd barely made it back to the hostel, before I had jumped into my bed and broken down in heart wrenching sobs.

I couldn't believe how embarrassed I was today. I shouldn't have done it. I shouldn't have!

Jamal had offered to console me but I didn't feel too safe with him alone in my room, and Amarachi was not done with her class. I'd sent her a few texts about what happened but she hadn't replied.

"Where are you, Amara?" I sobbed. I needed her hug so badly

Just then, I heard a soft knock on the door. Oh! She's finally back!

I speedily went and pushed open door, and almost fainted with shock when I saw Richard standing in front of me, with his hands in his pockets.

"What... Why are you here?" I whispered as he let himself in without my permission. So fast, he occupied all the space in the room. I suddenly felt suffocated, and he was the one suffocating me.

Where is his rubbish girlfriend?!

I placed my arms over my chest in a protective gesture as I watched him scan my room, before turning back his dark, hot gaze to me. I sucked in a breath as our eyes clashed.

"Why did you lie about me being your boyfriend? What gave you the idea that you could do that?" He asked in a low tone. I could see that he was very angry at me. I was angry at him too. He could have saved me the embarrassment by just ignoring and not talking to the wicked lecturer, but he hadn't. Instead he had openly denied me. Making me look like a freak.

"You have no right to question me! You monkey! Get out of my room or I'll call the police!" I yelled at him.

"I won't leave till you tell me why you lied! Tell me!" He yelled back with full force. I felt so infuriated that I didn't even care that the tears were rolling down my face now, I was so furious with him and I couldn't stop my self as I speedily moved closer to him and punched him with all the Power I could summon from my fists.

"You're the one who caused this mess in the first place, Richard! Tell me why I can't stop thinking about you?!"

"You... Think about me?"

"Yes! Yes, Richard! I think about you all the time! And I don't fucking know why I do that because I hate you! I hate how arrogant you are! I hate how you make me feel things I've never felt before! I hate that you—"

He kissed me.

I gasped his lips fell onto mine with a sensation so powerful that my knees felt mushy under me.

My eyes widened as I realized what had just happened. Richard was kissing me. Oh my God!

No words were uttered, just the sounds of our lips clashing together as he kissed me with so much heat that it stole my breath away.

I moaned as his hands snaked around my waist, pulling me flush against his strong body. He was so tall, I had to tiptoe to catch his lips and put my fingers through his soft, curly hair.

We were both too occupied to hear the movement at the door step.

"Wow! So I can't have fun with my boyfriend here, but you can make out with one motherfuck—"

Amarachi stopped the moment we broke apart and she was able to see Richard's face.

"OMG! RICHARD GENTRY!!!" She screamed.

****

CHAPTER SEVEN

✱ Sansa*

"OMG! RICHARD GENTRY!!" My lovely friend screeched from the front door, before jumping into the room with lightening speed.

I quickly jumped out of Richard's embrace as we all stared at each other, Amarachi gazing at him as if she were studying a painting, while Richard stared at me with the same expression I was almost too sure I had on my face; utter shock.

I shook my head slightly in denial of what had just simply happened. We'd been kissing. Passionately. And I'd even urged him on, forgetting my phobia for being touched by a male.

Why did this happen?? Why did I even let it happen?! What is wrong with me?!

Then my eyes involuntarily widened as I realized why this was happening. I was attracted to Richard. Not just a casual type of attraction, I was crazy about him. It finally explained why he seemed to consume my every sleeping and waking thoughts, the nervousness I felt when he was around me, the worry I felt when he was away.

I like Richard. Because, it definitely couldn't be love. I couldn't be in love with someone like him, someone who didn't mind hurting anybody that stood in his way. No. Not love. Lust, maybe.

"Richard! Oh my God! I get to finally see you!" Amarachi kept blabbering on, not even noticing the tension between me and the brooding Richard Gentry.

"Amarachi!" I snapped in a whisper as I pulled her slightly away, "Would you keep that your loud voice down? The whole building could be hearing you right now!"

"AND SO WHAT? RICHARD GENTRY IS FINALLY IN MY ROOM!"

I instinctively placed my hands over my ear with a wince as Amarachi kept on displaying her Banshee skills.

"Amara, please.. Can you give me a minute? I need to talk to him so he can leave peacefully." I urged in a pleading tone, hoping she'd listen.

"Oh! I should leave so you guys can swallow each other up abi?"

I sighed and silently glared at her.

She wiggled her eyebrows at me with a soft laugh, "Okay, okay, I've heard. But you must gist me sha oh!"

I watched her buttocks jiggle as she stalked to our tiny closet, throwing us each a dramatic glare before closing the door silently.

I let out a ragged breath before turning back to him.

"Why did you kiss me?" I simply asked. My voice soft.

"You were talking too much. Something had to shut you up, and that came into my head. Any other questions?" he probed.

"You... You.. You arrogant animal!"

"Watch what you say, Sansa—"

"No! I only work for you, Richard. You have no right to my personal space!" I yelled at him angrily. "I'm sorry I lied to my lecturer about you, but I only did that because he was trying to blackmail me. I don't like you and frankly, I want nothing to do with a sadist like you!"

I pressed my lips shut as I realized I had just named him a sadist. That was wrong. I shouldn't have, but I couldn't take the words back now. And I knew by the fierce scowl he had on his face, that he was extremely furious.

He smirked before stepping closer and stopping right in front of me.

"How many men have you slept with, Sansa?"

I flinched as if I'd just been slapped hard across the face. If I'd been slapped, I was sure I wouldn't be as shocked as I was now. All the color drained away from my face and neck as I stared hard at him.

"What.. What did you just say?" I whispered, my breath held tightly.

"I know your type. You pretend like you're some.. Innocent little princess, but you silently try to seduce unsuspecting men.. Like the lecturer, am I right?"

I couldn't believe my ears. I knew Richard was a cruel person, but this, this was too far.

"And now," He continued, "You tried to seduce me and formed the victim. So, I'm asking.. How many men have gotten under you, princess?"

At his mention of 'princess', I saw red and unconsciously tried to raise my right hand to slap him across the face, but I wasn't fast enough as he grabbed a hold of my wrist to stop me effectively.

"That is not something I would advise you to do, princess. I do not take hits lightly." He simply stated, smirking at me with satisfaction.

To my mortification, the tears I was trying to hold back was let loose. I felt like my heart was suffocating. I felt shamed and ridiculed. I couldn't continue to look at him.

"You're a bastard! Let me go!" I sobbed hoarsely as he finally set my wrist free. Without turning back, I dashed into the bathroom and locked the door, placing my palms over my mouth to subdue the horrible sounds that I couldn't believe were coming out of me.

I distinctively heard the angry voice of Amara as she was telling him the leave.

After a few minutes of silence, I jumped in fright at the knock on the door.

"Sansa, baby? He's gone now. Open the door, darling."

Without the slightest hesitation, I pushed open the door and jumped into Amarachi's warm, waiting arms, trembling with the force of my miserable sobs.

"It's okay, baby girl.. Let it out.." Her sweet, calming voice swayed like she wanted to cry too, which made me cry harder.

****

Richard

My eyes hurt. Keeping them open and trying to blink them was an effort.

I had never felt this way before. I had never felt this helpless and miserable. It was because of her. Sansa.

What is she doing to me? Why did she come into my life??

I sighed and placed my head exhaustingly on the drink counter. I had left her place and drove straight to my favorite club house after texting Folake that I wouldn't be able to take her home.

I checked my wrist. 7:25PM. I'd been here, drinking for over four hours, thinking about how hurt Sansa had been when I'd said those harsh words. I'd said it to make her angry, the way she equally made me angry.

Damn it! She literally knew how to drive someone mad without even trying! She'd called me a sadist, All Because I had mistakenly kissed her! A kiss she had returned with fervency, only if she was a pretender.

"Hi,"

I turned to the lady who stood before me, smiling like her life depended on it.

"What do you want?" I enquired impatiently. I was quite annoyed right now, I didn't need anyone fueling the fire.

"My name is Chelsea, I'm the chairman's daughter. I just recently resumed into Gentry University." She introduced.

That was why her face looked a bit familiar. She was one of the girls who had bullied Sansa at the eatery.

I studied her loud features. Her top had an unnecessary large slot in the middle, putting half of her big breasts on display, while she had on a short skirt that was meant to seduce any living thing. It didn't move me.

"I'm not interested in having Pep talks with you, girl. Get out." I mumbled before turning back to my drink.

"What do you see in her? That.. Stupid Sansa girl. She's not worth it." Chelsea stated, scorn filling her voice.

"She's not a desperate bitch who stalks guys into a club just for validation and attention. Now, get the fuck out of my way."

She looked shocked as I swiftly let my self out of darkly lit room. I went into my car and sped off without a backward glance.

****

Violent scenes ahead...

Sansa

I WAS TRYING TO BREATHE, but I couldn't. The pain that flared across my lower body was too much too bear, but I couldn't do anything about it.

The tears streamed down my face as they continued to violate my body, giving me injuries that would smear my life and taint my soul.

"Please," I gasped immediately my mouth was free. "stop," I tried to bring in mouthfuls of air. "Painful,"

God I want to die! God let me just die! Please!

I was tied into an unmovable position, spreaded in the worst way possible. I stared at them in horror, but I couldn't mutter a word. My mouth was filled with all sorts of rubbish. Semen, saliva, blood and the ones I couldn't point out.

It was too big for my mouth. My lips were horribly swollen, But I had no choice but to take it in. The pain, the horrible taste. I lied there as he and his friend did all they pleased on my body.

I had long since forgotten about my father. knowing him, he wouldn't be home. He wouldn't even remember I existed. He didn't even know that his kid nephew brought his friend along to torture me.

Wack! My head turned violently with the force of the slap I received. But I didn't react, I wouldn't react. I refused to give them the pleasure of watching me scream and cry in pains.

Everything felt numb. My body felt numb, even though I could feel the painful force of what they were doing to me, I couldn't react. I was too exhausted. I could only wait and wish for death to take me. Any second now, but it never came.

"You're forming strong girl for us abi?" Godwin whispered as he bit my ear hard, making me squirm from the piercing pain. He kept thrusting into me, faster and faster, till I couldn't keep track of the pace.

"You don't want to scream for us, right princess?" His friend said as he kept pushing back and forth into my mouth.

I could feel their frustration, and somehow, it made me happy. They couldn't get a reaction out of me, no matter how they tried.

Then I heard someone's voice from the other end of the dark room. That voice was too familiar. So familiar that immediately I heard it, my whole body began to tremble with fear and trepidation.

"SANSA! NO! LET HER GO!"

It was Richard. Oh no! Richard knows!

What was he doing here?! My body began to regain it's consciousness, and the pain felt like it was doubling. No!

Godwin laughed at me, before pointing towards where Richard was.. I couldn't make out his figure, it was too dark. "You think your Richard can save you, princess? He will watch us fuck you over and over!"

And then, I screamed.

"RICHARD!!!!"

"Sansa! Sansa! Wake up! Jesus christ! What's happening??"

My body jerked with the force of my scream as I jumped up in bed, Amarachi instantly by my side, trying to calm me down. She tried to place her hands on my shoulders, but I couldn't stop screaming and shaking on my bed.

"Richard! Amarachi.. They.. Richard.. He.. They raped me! Richard is in trouble! They will kill him!" I screamed frantically, grabbing Amarachi as she stared at me, her eyes widening with confusion.

"No! Nobody raped you! It was just a nightmare! Calm down!" She grabbed my tear-stricked face. "Look at me, Sansa. You're fine. You're fine."

"Noooo! No! Amara. You.. You don't understand! My cousin, he... He and his best friend hurt me!" I grabbed her arms, sobbing and trying to make her understand.

"Oh my God!" Amarachi gasped. The tears were rolling down her face now, she looked so furious and hurt at my revelation.

"Who did it to you? I will kill him! He must—"

"No! No! Amara.. Please.. Richard, I need to see him. He must be in danger! Please! Please!" I couldn't control my tears and my runny nose. My whole body was trembling violently, and I could still see the nightmare happening vividly before me, how they forced Richard to watch while they did their evil deed. No!

Amarachi tried to calm me down, but I kept crying, Trying to block out the horrible images of me being abused like a worthless doll.

"Sansa, please stop crying!" Amarachi sobbed, "You're making me cry as well, I don't know what to do to make you stop crying!"

I felt the rush of her heartbeat, and I knew that she was terrified by my reaction. She had never seen this side of me.

"Should we take you to the school hospital?" She asked, her voice breaking in between her tears.

I shook my head no, I kept on crying in her arms. I didn't know how to control my self. I knew now that everything was all a pretense. I couldn't ever get past what my cousin had done to me. He had destroyed my mental health, He had broken me. Over and over again. God!

I didn't realize that Amarachi had picked up my phone until she had raised the phone to her ear, calling someone.

She looked straight at me, her blood red eyes determined as she waited for whoever she was calling, to pick up.

As distressed as I was, I couldn't help the shocked gasp that broke out of me the moment I heard her statement.

"Hello?... This is Sansa's friend. Amara. Please, Richard. I need you to come here right now. Please,"

CHAPTER EIGHT

✱ Richard*

I hit the horn with enough force to break the device. I was going to loose it any second now, if the stupid security man didn't get this blasted gate open.

My hands were trembling with fear for Sansa. I kept trying to stop myself from imagining the worst that could have happened to her.

The moment I had gotten that tensed phone call from her roommate, I knew something was wrong. All the anger I'd kept in store had instantly evaporated and I found myself driving like a mad man straight to Sansa's school. I didn't care if she wasn't willing to see me. I needed to see her. For the sake of my own peace of mind.

"Who dey there! No body fit pass gate at this time oga! Abeg dey turn back now now!" The gate security yelled from the other side.

I turned on my car light and pushed the horn again with more force, until he came out, probably to shout at me some more. I waited till he was in front of me before winding down my windscreen.

His eyes widened as he took me in. I knew he had recognized my face. I scowled at him as he struggled with words.

"Em.. Sir.."

"Just open the gate and let me pass Ode" I commented as I watched him fiddle around, probably wanting to apologize.

"Okay sir." He replied hurriedly as he ran back and opened the gate. Without wasting more time, I sped up into the school compound, I made sure to park in front of Sansa's block.

I glanced up and saw some heads already popping out. These stupid students weren't asleep. Damn. I didn't care, I just had to get to Sansa.

I made my way over to her room, knocked lightly on the door and waited. No response. I knocked again. No response.

I was about to ponce on the door when it was pulled open. I stared at Sansa's friend. She looked.. Terrified.

"Where's Sansa?" I asked impatiently.

"Well.. There's.. There's an issue." I noticed she had slightly moved out and closed the door behind her.

"What issue do you mean? What's wrong with Sansa??" I queried.

"She.. She doesn't want to see you, Richard. I'm sorry- I shouldn't have bothered to call you.."

"I'm going to see her and none of you can stop me."

Without hesitating, I shoved her out of my way and pushed into the small, warm room. I stilled as I took in her form.

She was all curled up on her bed, her arms wounded tightly about her, and she seemed to be chanting something like 'It's not real, it's not real'.

My eyes scanned her figure. She was only in her underwear, which was kind of transparent, but my mind was not in that direction. I walked over to where she was.

It took a few moments before she fully realized that I was there. In front of her.

"What are you doing here?!" she screamed and turned to her friend who was pacing back and forth, her face wet with tears and sweat. "Amara! I thought I told you not to let him in!"

"I had no choice! You were asking for him! And there was no other way to calm you down than to call him!" Amara replied, her voice breaking with exhaustion.

Sansa turned to face me, a frown on her forehead. "I.. I'm sorry.. I just.." Without waiting for to finish her mumbling, I stooped down and gathered her into my arms.

Relief broke through me as she instantly welcomed my embrace and wrapped her hands tight around my neck. Neither of us said a word. Not a single movement. All I just wanted was to keep on holding tight against me, I wanted to see her vulnerable side. I wanted to watch the emotions fly out of her. This girl that both fascinated me and frustrated me.

After some minutes, she stopped trembling. My hand instinctively dropped from her neck, where it was. I'd been stroking her there, trying to ease off the tension.

I now realized that her friend, Amarachi had left the room. Probably to give us the privacy we didn't necessarily ask for. I wanted to chuckle but I knew it was not the right time.

Placing my finger under her chin, I slowly pulled her face up to meet mine. I stared into her dark brown eyes. Even though she had cried her eyes out, they still looked enchanting.

"Will you tell me what caused.. All this?" I asked slowly, not wanting to frighten her.

"Um..." Her voice sounded cracked and weak, it almost made me shudder. She shook her head slightly as she started to move away from my embrace, I held her back, my stare intent.

"Tell me." I commanded.

****

Sansa

My limbs were trembling with fear and trepidation. I didn't know what to say to Richard. I wanted to hit my head on the hard wood for not being able to control myself after having a nightmare.

I knew it had been awhile before I had seen those horrible nightmares, but most times, when it happened, I usually drank to take it off my chest.

But this... It had been so scary, so real. The fear and shame I'd felt when I saw Richard's tortured face still washed through me.

"I'm still waiting.." I heard his voice and turned to look at him. His features looked strained and worried and I felt my heartstrings pull for him, he was worried for me. Or was it just a lie?

"Well... I usually have those.. Nightmares. But.. I'll be fine." I murmured, my eyes looking down in shame. I couldn't tell him my situation, what had happened to me. I knew he would see me another type of way. Like a used, damaged doll.

"What was it about?" He asked, clearly not wanting the subject to be dropped.

"Nothing.. Really.."

"Did someone attack you, Sansa?"

I flinched immediately I heard the word 'attack'. It is more than that.

I clamped my mouth down as I stared at his beautiful, flawless face. His lips was so close to mine and I momentarily imagined how it would feel to kiss him. Again.

He'll say i seduced him again.

"Look... Thanks for coming here but I don't need you here. The last time you came here, you threw horrible words at me. So I don't know why you think we'd be good with each other." I accused as I set my palms firmly over his wide chest to push him away.

He didn't budge. He just smirked at me like he was amused. I still couldn't believe that I wasn't feeling scared by being so close to him. Maybe because I wanted him to be close to him. I liked this guy. So much.

"You look like you want to kiss me, angel." he whispered, amused. He was staring at my lips as well.

"The last thing I would do is kiss you. Not after the words you threw at me earlier. If you try to kiss me, I'll slap you. Standard." I didn't know where the sudden confidence was coming from, but I was glad. I wouldn't let him push me around.

"Alright, I apologize. I shouldn't have said those words to you. I won't say it next time."

"Next time?" I asked with a frown. "Who told you that there would be a next time?"

"Of course there would. Like now."

My eyes widened as I realized what he meant. I closed my eyes as i felt his lips crash onto mine.

This was the second time we were kissing in a day. Jesus.

Chapter Nine

Richard (Pov)

As I moved my lips more firmly into hers, I held back the urge to pinch myself. I was tempted to, because I couldn't quite believe that we were kissing. And she was responding in the most fascinating way. The soft sighs and moans that escaped her lips whenever we took a second to let some air in was like music to my ears. We both drew closer and the next thing I knew, she was there. In my arms. I pulled her further into myself and pushed her legs slightly apart, placing them on each sides of my hips, letting her straddle me so she could feel how turned on I was because of her.

She let out another soft, ragged moan, making me smile with satisfaction. "Can you feel me? Feel what you do to me?" I whispered into her ear as she trembled slightly with desire.

"Richard..."

Before she could say another word, I locked my lips unto her again. Deepening the kiss. We were both so lost in each other that we failed to notice the shadow that was right in front of us. We paused as we heard the sound of a camera click before the flashlight came on. We pulled away as we heard Amarachi, Sansa's friend and roommate giggle excitedly.

"Amara! What the hell are you doing?!" Sansa demanded angrily as she glared at her friend. She was already out of my arms and sitting on the other side of the bed. How did she get there??

"Oh my God! See how hot you two look! You were literally eating each other up, I just had to take a pic." Amarachi screeched, clapping her hands together.

"What? No. Amarachi delete that right now!" Sansa said as she got up and made to drag the phone out of Amarachi's hand. But she wasn't fast enough.

"Why would you want me to delete it? Here. Take a look at how lovely you both look." Amarachi flashed the phone in Sansa's face. I watched as they studied the pic with a smile on my face.

"It's nice but you still have to delete it, Amara." Sansa begged, trying to pull the phone out of her friend's hands.

"Ah ah, why do you want it deleted so bad?" Amarachi queried.

"Because.. Well... You have so many friends in class that could mistakenly see it!"

"That's even better. I'll show those bitches that embarrassed you. I'll watch how they will be speechless and jealous..."

"No! You can't do anything like that! Nobody must know that this guy entered my room, or that we kissed. Please, Amara" Sansa pleaded desperately.

"And why does it bother you so much if we're seen kissing?" I asked, walking over to where she was with a frown. "Is there a particular reason why you don't want us to be seen together?"

Sansa turned to me with a glare. I chuckled slightly. I was convinced that the girl was bipolar. One minute she was crazy about me, the next she looked like she couldn't wait to kill me finish. "Simply because, I have nothing to do with you. Yes I may be attracted to you, and may have made the mistake of kissing you.. Just for the fun of it, but asides that, I have nothing with you, Richard Gentry. Get out now and go and attend to your girlfriend in peace."

I smiled at her expression. She wanted to believe that she hated me so bad, but she couldn't fool me. She wanted me. She just wouldn't admit it to herself no matter what.

"You're my girlfriend, starting from now." I stated with an impressive grin.

"You are mad." Sansa replied. I put out my hands to stop her as she was about to walk away but stopped when she slightly staggered. I caught her quickly before she could hit the ground. I looked down to check what could have caught her feet but then, I noticed how she was breathing heavily. She was very weak.

"Sansa? Are you alright?" I asked nervously, scooping her into my arms before walking back to bed, Amarachi beside me.

"Um.. Yeah. Just feeling a little light headed." She whispered, placing a hand on her forehead.

"She needs to eat." Amarachi suggested.

"No, no.." Sansa replied softly. "I just need... Sleep. I feel dizzy. Amarachi, please make this guy go away. He mustn't sleep with us."

"You heard her." Amarachi deadpanned as she glared at me.

"I'm not leaving until I can confirm she's okay. Go get her water and stop glaring at me with those chicken eyes." Sansa chuckled at my words, before resting her head onto the pillow.

Minutes later, Sansa was sound asleep. I watched carefully as she breathed slowly, in and out. I took the opportunity to study every single detail of her. From the long wave of eyelashes that rested slightly on her high cheekbones, to the hairs on her arm and legs, an incredibly soft and delicate skin, then her chest moving slightly up and down. The girl was too beautiful for her own good. I didn't understand how she didn't have men moving mountains for her by now.

"Why don't you just make it official and ask her out?" I turned and saw Amarachi smiling knowingly at me. I stared at her for a moment before turning back to Sansa.

"It's so clear that you care about her. Just saying though,"

"She's too young and innocent for this. I'd prefer her to be protected. And if she's with me... I can't guarantee that." I explained silently, still watching Sansa.

"Why?"

"Hard to explain."

"Richard, why do you think she had such a terrifying nightmare?" Amarachi asked. I could hear the worry in her quivering voice.

"I'm still trying to figure that out." I replied.

She moved closer to me and placed her hand on my shoulder, making me turn to look at her questioningly.   "Richard,... I really have this deep feeling in my gut," She paused as if she was too scared to continue. I think

I was too. "That something really bad has happened to Sansa in the past. This is not a normal reaction. It's like she's a time bomb whenever I'm with her. It's like she's being haunted by an evil figure. I just.. I just can't understand what it is."

"Amarachi, I swear... I would find out what's happened with her. I will." I promised softly. I noticed the moisture in her eyes as she smiled at me gratefully with a soft nod of her head. I nodded too.

****

I slowly opened my eyes before glancing at my watch. It was past 3. I turned to look at the sleeping beauty beside me. I noticed she was more relaxed now. She was snoring softly and one of her legs was raised up in an awkward position, making me chuckle. I took a moment before getting up.

"You're leaving?" Amarachi asked, her eyes focused on her phone.

"Yes. You want me to stay?" I demanded jokingly.

"This building will be brought down if Sansa wakes up and finds you here. So, you can go." She said, smiling slightly.

I smiled and picked up my jacket, phone and wallet before making my way out of the room.

"Oh and one more thing, Richard." I stopped but didn't turn. I waited. "I know you're... Mr hotshot, but I want you to know that Sansa is my friend and I will watch out for her. So whatever your intention for is, it better be good."

"What do you mean?" I turned to her, confused.

"What I mean is... If you hurt Sansa in any type of way, I will do everything in my power to make sure you regret it. Understood?"

I kept quiet and stared at her defiant face for what seemed like hours. Then I gently nodded my head and silently walked out.

Chapter Ten

S ansa (Pov)

A week later, we were all getting ready for our matriculation program. There was going to be a big party right after the program and that was what got us excited. Especially Amarachi.

"I'm going to set the dance stage on fire! That's why I bought these fish nets" Stephanie, a friend of Amarachi said with full excitement as she dangled the tiny pieces in front of our faces.

"Omo, my own na to drink to the fullest. I'm finna get drunk!" Tinu, another friend of Amarachi quipped.

"Yeahhhh!" The girls screamed excitedly. I sighed. Amarachi had introduced 3 of her other friends to me earlier this morning, Stephanie, the one that was exactly like her, Tinu, her course rep, then Damilola, her project partner. Damilola was the gentle one and I knew I could get along with her better.

"What do you plan on doing after the party, Sansa?" Damilola asked, her voice sounded very childish and adorable.

"I don't really know. I think I'll just come back to the hostel cause I don't really fancy all these parties and dancing stuff.."

She smiled slightly and nodded. "Well.. I think.. For the first time, I'll be spending the night with my boyfriend." She concluded with a funny look on her face.

I slowly nodded my head awkwardly and kept quiet. I had no idea why she thought I needed to know that piece of information so I pretended as if I didn't know what she meant.

"Hey, Sansa?" Amarachi called from the other side of the room. "Please come check this fit for me now o, before you say I'm dressed like a mad woman for the party."

I headed over to her with a soft shake of my head. Amara knew how much I detested doing things like this but I had no choice. "What's the color of your outfit?" I enquired, trying to hide the disinterest in my voice.

"Gold and black. But.. I just feel like it's..."

"The combination is perfect to me, I also think it would go with your skin color well." I quickly concluded. She glowered at me with a funny look on her face before turning to reveal the dress. It was a very beautiful dress, but not the kind I would wear. Mine was just a simple dark gown made of suede. Nothing special.

I turned to leave her to herself before she stopped me with a hand on my upper hand. "What's wrong?"

"I know you don't like me meddling, but I'd just like to know your situation with Mr hotshot."

I felt my face flame up. I immediately knew who she was referring to, but I pretended not to. "I don't know any 'hotshot' You're talking about, and I certainly do not have any situation."

"You do. With Richard Gentry. I mean... The whole campus knows about it. How much longer do you guys want to keep acting like there's really nothing between you two?" She asked, her face creaking with a frown. I sighed and tried to fix my gaze on anything else but her. I didn't know what to say.

"Well... I.. I'm attracted to him. And that s normal because he's a good looking guy. Any sane girl would feel the same way about him."

"That's not the point and you know it."

"What's the point?"

"Sansa, have you forgotten what happened last week? the guy literally calmed you down with just a kiss after you had a crazy fit. That one is normal my sis,"

I frowned and thought about it as well. What was it about that guy that made me a better version of. Myself? He made me feel things I didn't think I was capable of feeling. Things I thought had been damaged by my evil cousin. He made me excited with just a look, he made me frustrated, he made me hot and bothered and as much as I wanted to deny it, he made me happy, especially after what had happened last week. I could hardly even remember what happened through out the week except that he spent almost every night in my hostel after that night I had the nightmare. Talking with me and sometimes Amara. I chuckled as I recalled how they'd argued and bantered with each other the previous night. I'd almost cracked my ribs from laughing too much.

"Look.. Amara, I don't know what exactly is going on between the two of us, and I'm not about to find out. Can we just leave this topic and Enjoy our matric please? All I want to do today is to eat jollof rice."

"Hmm... Okay ooo,"

LATER IN THE DAY, all the 100 level students and newbies were gathered in the general hall where all kinds of amazing programs were going on. As we walked into the hall, me and Amarachi with her friends, I silently pushed away the anxiety that was eating at my soul from being around so many people. The last thing I wanted was a panic attack in public. I wouldn't live that down for as long as I was in this school.

I felt a hand grab mine steadily. I turned and saw Amara smiling sweetly at me.   "Take deep breaths. In and out, slow and steady. You'll be fine my love,"

I nodded with a grateful smile on my face. Amarachi was a God sent and I was super lucky to have her.

"Do you know how pretty you look? People are looking at you, Sansa. I want you to relax and enjoy yourself. Make more friends, dance and take pictures. I'll be right by your side if you have any problems. I promise."

My throat closed up as I felt my eyes start to constrict. I nodded slightly, not knowing what to say. I couldn't understand why or how she was kind to me. It wasn't like I deserved it. "Amara, I don't even know how to thank you..."

"Thank me by finally agreeing to give Richard that coochie—"

"Amara!" I stopped her before she could go any further and embarrass me. "Will you Stop saying rubbish things like that?"

"What! Oh you want to deny that you've never imagined how he looks down there? Or how it'll feel if he—"

"Okay just shut up! Now!" I said with a loud gasp. This girl was something else. I heard the sound of laughter as I walked away and into the nearest bar. I quickly grabbed a bottle of soft drink and downed it desperately. Suddenly, I felt a movement behind me which made me tensed. Was it Richard??

"Hello," I turned, heat burning in my cheeks as I faced a total stranger. "Hi," I replied shakily.

"I hope you don't mind me joining you? I just wanted to take a minute to appreciate your beauty." the guy stared at me with a lustful look in his eyes.

I was about to give him a rude reply when I heard Amarachi's voice echo in my head. I bit down on my lip and tried to form a smile on my lips. "Um… Thank you."

"May I know your name, pretty girl?"

"Sansa."

"Sansa, can I get your number? We should talk some other time."

I wordlessly glared at the guy as he kept smiling back at me. Is this how to toast a girl? Mumu

"Malik, she isn't giving you a reply maybe you should get the message and leave her be."

I turned to see another guy, who I didn't know, standing on my left hand side. He was looking at the other guy with a look of warning in his eyes. Omo.

"Look, you guys should carry your wahala and go abeg, my boyfriend is around the corner and I'm sure you don't want me to tell you who he is." I said, a sly smile slowly forming on my face.

The two of them stared at me confusingly before the first guy stepped back suddenly. A surprised look on his face. My smile widened. "You're the girl that is following Gentry?" He asked in an incredulous voice. I watched them silently. They looked like a ghost was in front of them. It was too fun to watch.

"Are you going to leave or will you wait him to come and meet you here?" I taunted.

I released my breath as they hurriedly walked away. They didn't seem like a threat to me but I wasn't going to take any chances. The only person I could let my guard down with was Richard Gentry. Amarachi was right. I was developing feelings for him. And I couldn't figure out how or why it was even happening. You are supposed to not have a heart anymore. Isn't that what we agreed on?

Just then, I felt a light tap on my shoulder and turned to see Ayomide. My coworker. He smiled at me and moved to give me a hug, which I received warmly.

"Ayo! Such a pleasant surprise to see you! Though I'm wondering what you're doing at our school. Are you here for the matric?"

"Well, not really. I'm just here with my younger sister. She's the one having the matric." He replied enthusiastically. The excitement clear on his face.

"Oh, your sister is here in this school? That's nice. Where's she?"

"Right now she's with her friends. I was actually just supposed to drop her off and leave immediately, but I really couldn't waste the opportunity to see you. Especially in this.. Exquisite gown you're in. You look so beautiful, Sansa."

I felt the heat rise in my cheeks as I smiled at him. "Thank you. You don't look bad, yourself."

He chuckled before taking my hand in his and directing me towards a more discreet area of the hall. "I was hoping we could get a chance to talk a bit. That's if you're interested, my dear."

"No, she's not interested uncle. Now you can get back to work." Amarachi stated before I could give a reply. I turned to her with a glare before giving Ayomide an apologetic smile.

"I'll be right back, just let me say something to my friend." I told him before dragging Amara to the end or the room.

"What was that about??" I demanded, my voice higher than it was supposed to be.

"No. Let me ask you, what is that about?? You're clearly flirting with that clown over there and you're asking me what it is about?" She exclaimed.

"Since when do you decide who I talk with? Where were you when two guys were practically jumping me the other time?!" I questioned annoyingly.

"Oh please! I saw how well you handled them. They were almost shitting their pants as they ran away from you. You didn't need my help. But this," she pointed to Ayomide, who was studying us from the end of the room. "He wants to jump you, and you're giving him hand. Didn't you tell him about Richard?"

"Amara, sometimes you talk like you smoked something hard. The guy is just my friend and Richard is not my boyfriend! Get that in your head and let me be for goodness sake!"

"I'm going to sit beside you. I want to know what you guys are talking about." Amara said, her mouth squeezed together so stubbornly. What was I going to do with her?

"Fine. Have it your way. We're talking about nothing else than work so you might as well bore yourself to hell."

I turned back and went to meet Ayo, Amara following closely behind me. "Sorry for my friends rude behavior, she's just...."

"I'm looking out for my friend and I don't care who you are, uncle" Amara piped in. The defensive tone in her voice made me want to laugh hard and also beat her with frustration.

"Of course, Miss Amarachi. Nice to meet you. And.. It's good, the way you look out for your friend Sansa..."

At that moment, my phone vibrated. I turned on the screen and my heart skipped when I saw who it was.

"Meet me at the school square in 20 minutes, do not be late."

I unconsciously placed my hand on my racing heart to try and stop the excitement that was building there because I knew who it was. I turned to look at Amarachi. She was staring at me with a wide, knowing grin.

Chapter Eleven

Sansa (Pov)

I let out a shaky breath. Richard wanted to see me and I was going to see him. I could barely hide the excitement that was threatening to burst out of me As I said a quick goodbye to an equally excited Amarachi and a confused looking Ayomide. I couldn't blame him though, the way I was acting confused me myself. I didn't wait to convince my self otherwise, instead I just jumped into the first cab I saw outside the school hall.

After a few minutes, the cab stopped right in front of the school square. I let out a deep exhale as I stepped out of the cab. From where I was standing, I could see Richard's black Lamborghini shining in the night. It was already dark. In front of the car, was the man that owned it. I couldn't say a word. My throat was closed up as I made my way towards him. He had his hands in his pockets which made him look impossibly more sexy. Was that even a thing?

"Hi," I whispered. I could already feel the heat in my cheeks. Why couldn't I just control my feelings when I was around this guy?!

"You're one minute late. I should punish you." He said in a low growl, making me smile unconsciously.

"You're even lucky I left my party and my friends to come meet you. So tell me what you want now so I can get back to my people."

"You need to reduce that rude tone in your voice else I'll kiss it away." He stated, making my eyes turn wide like a deer's. I took a nervous step back while he took one forward.

I didn't get the chance to figure out what he wanted to do before he roughly pulled me into him and lowered his head bringing my lips with his in a ruthless kiss. I let out a soft moan as I felt his hands circle my neck to deepen the kiss. I wrapped my hands around his shoulder, pulling him closer. I'd somehow forgotten that we were in public, or I just simply didn't care.

"I love how sweet and innocent you look when I kiss you," He said in a soft whisper. I felt his sweet breath fan all over my face.

"Richard... Someone might see.."

"Let them see. Don't you understand how you affect me? Do you know how much I want you? How I want to feel your naked body against mine? How I want to hear the sweet sound of you moaning out my name? I want you so badly, Sansa."

The rhythm of his words froze me in place as soon as I understood what he meant. He wanted me in a way that could never be possible. I swallowed a hard breath as terror tore through my body, making me instantly pull away and turn my back towards him. Richard didn't know how damaged I was. If he knew, I was almost too certain that he would spit at me in disgust.

Who would want to have sex with a girl who was physically and sexually damaged? I shook my head tightly to blurt out the dirty images that were trying to make their way into my head.

"I want to sleep with you, Sansa" He confirmed flatly. I felt my heart break as I imagined how he would react when I finally told him that it wouldn't be possible. "But that's not just it," he continued, moving closer to stand in front of my back. "I also want to get to know you deeply, your secrets, your fears, your expectations. That's why I want you to get in the car with me. Lemme take you out. Please." He added after a second of silence.

I turned to him with a smile plastered on my face and shook my head. Without any more words, he led me to his car. We got in and the driver drove off.

****

Richard (Pov)

"So.... Can I ask where you're actually taking me?" Sansa asked, her voice barely more than a whisper.

"I'm not telling you ma'am, you'd just have to trust that I'm not out to kidnap or sell you or whatever is going through that mind of yours right now." I had the satisfaction of hearing her sweet giggle.

"It better not be that you're taking me to the office. It won't be funny because I'll change it for you." She warned, making me chuckle lightly.

We settled back into silence as the car moved on.

AFTER WHAT SEEMED LIKE HOURS, the car came to a stop. "We've arrived, Sir." The driver said. I turned to Sansa and saw the curiosity hidden in her eyes.

"Richard, where are we?"

"Come on," I pulled her with me and stepped out of my car. I watched as her eyes widened with so much fascination and excitement in them. She was looking every which way. "Do you like it?" I enquired silently. I didn't like the tone of nervousness I could hear in my voice, but there was nothing I could do to stop it. My feelings for this small, loudmouthed girl with troubles made me want to protect her. To make her happy in any way I could. My world was slowly revolving round her pinky finger.

"Oh my God! It's beautiful, Richard! How.. How did you do it?" She gasped.

I studied the scenery. I wasn't the type that used my money to impress a woman just because I wanted her. Women came to me without hesitation. But this, this was different. I wanted to make tonight special, just for her.

There was a swimming pool in the middle of the field, the lights were dim and just on the surface of the pool, stood a round table filled with all kinds of foods and drinks, with water proofed sofas on each sides of the table. The setting was made to look like we would be dining on water, which I knew was something that would impress any human being alive, even the stone-hearted Sansa. There was still that look of pure euphoria on her beautiful face. She was stuck staring at the magical looking scene, and I was stuck staring at her sheer beauty under the dimmed lights. It was now I noticed that she a small mole on the area close to her chin. Somehow that made her look even more beautiful to me.

"A good friend of mine helped with all the setup. All I had to do was tell him that I needed so badly to impress a girl." I explained as we walked hand in hand to the pool. There was a fleet of stairs in front of the swimming pool that would direct us to our spot.

"You must have spent... A lot on this. It looks too perfect. I don't know how anyone could even manage to make a place this beautiful." Sansa said, her tone light as ever.

"It's nothing compared to what I'd like to spend on you if you give me the chance to have you." I knew immediately the words came out that Sansa would take them wrongly. For some women, hearing a man say what I had just said would make them extremely happy, but for someone like Sansa... Judging by the expression on her face, she was completely pissed off.

"Where did you get the idea that I want you to spend your money on me?? Is that what all this is about?" She queried, motioning around us. "You think I want your money??"

"Calm down—"

"Which calm down! You just implied that you will spend money to get me in your bed. Do I look like some call girl to you??"

"Baby, that's not what I meant!"

"Don't call me your baby! In fact, Take me back to my school. Now."

I groaned out loud in frustration as she turned and stormed off. How did the night go from pleasant and romantic to this??

"Sansa, hold on!" I yelled, running after her. I took one step on the marble floor and slipped.

****

Sansa (Pov)

I heard the loud splash of water before I heard him shout. I turned around to find Richard thrashing and coughing, trying to get himself above the water.

"Richard!" I screamed.

"Sansa! Help! I'm not.. A swimmer!" He screamed, flinging his arms up like a wailing child. I ran over to where the he was and hastily pulled off my gown, revealing the lacy black panties and bra I was wearing. I quickly dashed into the water and swam over to him.

Swimming was one of my favorite activities. It helped those times when I used to have those uncontrollable panic attacks, I would just put myself in the jacuzzi for hours until my body returned to normal or I was almost dead. The last time it happened my father had found me, under water in my bathroom and lifeless. Somehow, he'd revived me and warned me off taking a bath in the jacuzzi.

"I'm coming! Hang on! Try not to drown." I urged as I got closer and closer to him. I noticed how hard he was trying to stay afloat. Damn him for bringing us to the largest swimming pool I had ever seen in my life.

I pushed forward with all the strength and speed I could gather, but just before I got to him, he went under. "Noo!" Taking in huge lumps of air, I went under water. Fortunately, he hadn't gotten too far when I grabbed him by his shoulder and lifted him up, above the water.

I gasped as I was able to finally let fresh air into my lungs. "Richard, Richard, are you okay?" I patted his face softly. His eyes were closed and I was having a hard time holding his large frame.

Suddenly, his arms came up around me as he pulled me tightly into him, making me gasp in shock. His eyes were wide open now, and he was smiling at me. Smiling at me!

"I thought you were.. I thought you drowned!" I exclaimed, licking my lips in confusion.

"Angel.. I said I'm not a swimmer, I didn't say I wasn't good at swimming." He replied amusingly. "Yes, I tricked you into thinking I was drowning, I needed to see that cute, angry face of yours"

"You... You.." I stuttered. I couldn't even find the words to describe him. He was the most impossible man on the planet. "You're mad!"

"Madly in love with you, Sansa."

We both froze in place as soon as the words came out. He was even more shocked than I was, his whole body was shaking. I didn't know if it was because of the cold water or because he had just confessed that he was in love with me.

"I..." my voice trailed off as we stared into each other's eyes. "Richard.. I.. I feel the same way too... But—"

Before I could go on, Richard kissed me softly on the lips. I realized that I had nothing on except bra and pant, which was extremely wet right now. Coupled with his wetness. I could feel every inch of his hard body against mine.

"Richard..." I said in between soft, wet kisses. "I need to tell you.." he took the opportunity and swept his tongue deep into my mouth, swallowing my words, and the kiss went on and on and on. Everything else faded, it was only me and him, and the sound of our lips locked passionately together.

Chapter Twelve.

Richard (Pov)

"The motive of this business idea is to create an awareness for our other competitors.." David Gentry, who was my father was speaking to the board members. I sighed exhaustedly, pulling up my sleeves to reveal my wristwatch. 3:22pm, it showed. I glanced up at my father who was still facing the table full of people and the way they were listening to him With rapt attention. We were in Ghana for a very important board meeting. My father had forced me to fly in from Nigeria.

"So now," My father continued, "I have decided that we should demolish the 4 closed streets with 5 storey buildings located somewhere in Accra." He finished.

"But Sir," one of the board members, a man who looked to be in his sixties spoke up, uncertainty written all over his wrinkled face. "The local government has kept a leash on that particular area of Accra. Wouldn't it cost a bit too much for us? because I understand that we will have to file an appeal before the land is open to us.."

"And moreover, there are people living in these areas you talk about demolishing... Families that depend on the place for their livelihoods. Are we supposed to just throw them out? I think you should rethink this decision Mr Gentry." That was Mrs Coker. She was a shrewd business woman but she was also considerate. She liked to do things to everyone's advantage. Unlike my father, his own desires overruled any compassion for the less privilege.

"As a matter of fact, I have thought about that and as we're filing an appeal for the takeover of the land, we'd be offering them millions for the severance."

"That was the same thing you did the last time father," I cut him off, sticking a foot awkwardly on the table. The board members turned to me with surprise. This was the first time I was mentioning a word since I started attending board meetings with my father.

"What do you mean, Richie?" My father demanded. I hated when he called me that.

"You said the same thing the last time." I repeated. "You acquired a land in a remote village in kano state, and paid a severance fee to the local government. What was heard months after?... People lost their family members to starvation and the ones that went to the forest to live were either attacked by deadly animals or never found again. People died, dad. All because you wanted to demolish a whole village. That's inhumane if you ask me."

"I agree," Few of the others chorused.

My father glared at me before nodding his head slowly. "So.. What do you all suggest we do?"

Mrs Coker cleared her throat and stood up. "There's a business proposal my company has for you sir, if you would just check it out, I'm certain it will be more favorable for you. For everyone of us, sir."

She turned to me with a slight smile on her face. Kind of like commending me for giving her the chance to present her project. I nodded back at her with a smile on my face as well. Just then, my phone vibrated.

I opened it to check who it was.

It was my firecracker. Sansa.

I miss you. Coming back when?   S.

Without hesitation or permission from my father, I got up and moved to the office close to the board room. I clicked on video call and waited until she picked up.

"Hey there, firecracker" I said immediately her beautiful face appeared on my screen.

"Will you Stop calling me that? I'm a gentle girl and you know it." Sansa asked, feigning a look of annoyance on her face.

"Gentle? Ha!" I snickered. "The last thing you are is gentle my dear. You literally pushed me into a whole pool the other day. A gentle girl wouldn't do things like that."

She gasped. "But I wasn't the one that pushed you, uncle. You were the one that jumped into it by yourself. Why do you always accuse me wrongly all the time!"

I chuckled at the expression on her face. She had her tied up almost close to her forehead, giving her that look of a 15 year old. I studied her mouth as it moved up and down as she kept ranting on. I still couldn't believe this girl was mine.

After we had kissed at the pool, I'd taken her back to her hostel and there we'd spent over two hours talking and kissing. I hadn't dared to touch her inappropriately because I was scared of what her reaction would be.

I wanted her to be comfortable and to know that I would never do what she didn't want. I would wait for as long as she wanted because I knew she was different. Special.

"Are you even listening to me??!" She snapped, pulling me out of my thoughts. "Why did you now call me if you were going to just let me keep on talking to myself, mtchew"

I turned my head over, laughing uncontrollably. "See what I mean by firecracker? You too dey vex!"

"Shut up. I wasn't vexed. I was just..."

"We're having an important board meeting out there, and you're here talking to your side chicks." My father said from behind me.

"I'll call you back, hun. Take care." I said to Sansa before cutting the call. I turned back to my father with a glare. "What do you mean by side chicks?" I demanded.

My father chuckled lightly before shaking his head and leaning forward to place his hand on my shoulder. "I have eyes and ears in the school, Richie. I know you're currently following a student of the school, and I know her name is Sansa Osaze. The reason why I didn't bother to confront you about it was because I was certain she was just a mode of entertainment for you. But now, it looks like she's becoming a big distraction to you. Am I right?"

"I don't see how this concerns you father, and just a fair warning, don't you dare go near her. You did that with my last girlfriend and I let you get away with it, because she didn't mean anything to me. If you try it this time.. You will regret it. I promise sir. "

My father studied me for a few moments, then he bursted out, laughing. I felt the anger in me rise a notch higher. I could punch the man any moment from now.

"Oh Richie, my son. You make me laugh. Your last girlfriend was a slut and you blame me for that?" he asked, still laughing. "It's not my fault that she was too greedy and wanted to have a taste of father and son. And it won't be my fault if this... Sansa of yours wants the same thing. I'll give it to her just how she would like it—"

I didn't wait for him to finish. I grabbed him by the neck and yanked him over. "If you dare touch her, I'll kill you. I swear. Don't make the mistake of setting your eyes on her. And tell your guards and security men that if I catch them stalking her, they will be killed on the spot." I shoved him away, making him stagger and almost hitting the wall before standing straight up.

"You dare raise your hand on me son?" He whispered, his voice deadly.

"What I should have done when you humiliated mom in front of the whole world. You cheated on her with girls young enough to be your grand daughters and I had to watch mom suffer in silence, not being able to do anything about it. Not anymore. I will not let you hurt anyone close to me, by God."

I turned and started walking out but my dad stopped me. "Maybe you don't know who the girl's father is. You have Google, use it and get back to me later."

Without anymore words, I walked out of the office and crashed into the board members. they were all standing in front of the door of the office. They scrambled awkwardly and backed away, embarrassed at being caught eavesdropping on the conversation with my father.

"I hope you all enjoyed the show," I commented with a laugh. "Meeting is over."

I stalked out of the room without a backward glance.

****

Sansa (Pov)

"So what do you say to that? Just you and me, with any type of Netflix series." Ayomide suggested cheerfully.

"Mm hmm," I nodded as if I was listening to him, but my mind was preoccupied with thoughts about Richard. How he had abruptly ended the call. I'd heard the voice of a man in the back ground just before he'd cut the call with a frustrated look on his face. My mind was telling that it was his father and my mind was telling me his father didn't like me.

"Or would you rather we go to the movies? Would that make you feel more comfortable?"

I didn't know why it mattered so much to me but I really hoped Richard's father didn't hate me. But to be honest, who would want a girl who has been raped and may have lost the ability to give birth in future? No one would. And how could I even explain this to Richard? He wouldn't understand. And even if he did.. I couldn't let him subject himself to that kind of life. Not having kids of his own, not seeing his wife pregnant for him. No, I couldn't. Sooner or later, I would have to end this relationship with him before it caused deeper damages.

"I'm talking to you and you're not even responding, it's not fair, Sansa." Ayomide's frustrated voice brought me out of my reverie. I turned to him.

"Oh, Ayo I'm So sorry. I was just thinking about... Richard." his face darkened with displeasure as soon as I mentioned his name.

"Do you like him?" He asked.

"I love him, Ayo." I replied.

"I see.." He looked away.

I felt bad for him, but I didn't want him to just keep making these unnecessary advances.

"Well.. I just hope you're happy. And be careful. He looks like the type of guy who could break your heart." He warned in a warm voice. I smiled gratefully at him.

"Thank you, Ayo. I appreciate it." I replied.

He stood up and left my office, leaving me alone. Finally. I quickly grabbed my phone and made to dial Richard's number when a knock came on the door.

"Who's that?" I demanded.

"Miss Sansa," it was the security man. "You have guests. She said she's your roommate and one other friend from your school."

"Oh! It's Amarachi and Jamal!" I spoke out, jumping off my chair in a hurry to get to the door. They'd promised they were going to visit me at my work place one of these days.

"Let them in!"

"Hey girlllllll" Amarachi screeched as she entered into my office, following behind a grinning Jamal. I gasped as I saw their arms filled up with all kinds of foods.

"Oh my God! You guys brought all these for me??" I asked, watching as they set everything on my table.

"Yes we did!" Amara replied excitedly. "We had food's day in class," Jamal explained, opening a box full of vegetable sauce. "So we decided to keep some for you and since you said you were lonely because your boyfriend traveled, we decided to bring them to you right here."

"Wow that's so nice! Thank you guys!" Amarachi was already stuffing her face with chicken, making me laugh at her.

"And here," Jamal reached into his bag and brought out a note book. "I also brought the assignment we were given for history. That's five marks."

"Thank you, Jamal. You're a life saver." I said, giving him a peck on the cheek as I collected the book.

"Uh uh. None of that pecking shit should happen beside me." Amarachi spat out, mouth full of chicken. "If not I'll report you to Gentry."

"You're not alright, ode." I laughed.

The sound of my phone ringing made me jump. "Oh! That must be Richard!"

"God when!" Amarachi Wined jokingly making me giggle.

But to my greatest surprise, it was not Richard. It was someone I hadn't expected to hear from in a while. I slowly pressed on the button to receive the call.

"Dad."

"Adesuwa," His voice was a soft purr from the other side of the phone. Like he'd been waiting to hear my voice. Like he was dying without it.

"What.. What do you want dad?"

"I want to see you, Adesuwa. I want to see my daughter."

I took in a deep breath and shut my eyes tightly. "Dad, I don't—"

"I want to see you now. I'm at your hostel and I'm waiting for you." his tone went from soft to hard.

"What?"

"I'm in front of your hostel right now. Don't keep me waiting dear daughter." He said sharply, before the line went off.

Chapter Thirteen

I took a deep breath as I got down from the cab in front of my hostel compound. I took each step as slowly as I could. I was nervous and angry and scared. I didn't want to see his face at all. The face of the man who took my precious mother from me. He was the reason I had left Lagos in the first place, I didn't want any connection to him and that is why I decided to apply for the scholarship that would take me far away from him.

I'd parted with Amarachi and Jamal on my way. They'd returned to class which I was supposed to do as well if not for the unexpected call I had gotten from that man.

"Are sure you don't want us to go with you Sansa? I don't think you should be left alone with him please..." Amarachi had said before we'd parted ways, her tone laced with so much worry.

"Don't worry, Amara. I promise I'll be fine. You and Jamal can go to class, I'll meet up with you. He's my father he won't harm me." I'd reassured both of them softly.

Amara had offered to come with one last time before leaving with Jamal, reluctantly. Now, walking into the hostel, I found myself wishing my friends were here with me. I couldn't trust myself not to say something terrible to the old man when I'm alone with him.

I knew something was off the moment I saw him leaning on the railings in front of my room. He looked.. Off somehow. Like he was sick. My father was hardly ever sick. Even though, I couldn't bring myself to worry about him. He was only my father in name, nothing else.

"Hello, Dad," I greeted quietly as I rounded up the corner and stood in front of him.

"Adesuwa, my lovely daughter..."

I blinked and quickly turned away, pretending to search for my keys before he could get the chance to embrace me. "It's hot outside.. We should head inside before the sun fries you up."

I heard his soft chuckle behind me as we entered the room. I shifted for him to make his way into the room, and stood in front of the door, not leaving it closed.

"What do you want Dad? Why are you here?" I demanded sharply.

He sighed. "I needed to see my girl, after all she has refused to take my calls or to even read my mails."

"I told you I'm fine but I needed that separation from you. What's wrong with that??" Sansa replied bitterly.

"I know that is why you ran all the way here, to be away from me. And you know that I could have stopped you if I so wished to, but I didn't. Because I wanted you to have your freedom. But that doesn't mean you will ignore my calls and texts, Adesuwa."

"Look, I'm always busy. I have to juggle work and school..."

"You work? What work is that? Why would you be working when you can have money as much as you want!"

"Oh, for God's sake..." I muttered under my breath, placing my fingers on my forehead in frustration.

"Adesuwa, what work do you do?" He questioned in a quiet voice.

"Just something to... Get me by. It's a decent work and I'm really enjoying it. Now can you leave?"

"At least you will tell me why you have refused to even check your mails. I had important news to tell you. Aliu as well."

I kept quiet and stared at him. We both exchanged looks before he gave up with a sigh and walked slowly over to the bed, like he was tired of standing.

"Are you okay?" I asked. He'd been looking sick since I saw him, I really wanted to act like I didn't care so bad, but i just wasn't that kind of person.

"No... I am not. You would have known this had you spared just a glance at my messages." He finished, his voice sounding too wary.

"What is wrong with you?" His eyes shot up to mine in shock, making me wince inwardly. Even I could hear how worried my voice sounded.

"I am... Sick." He muttered, looking away.

"What do you mean by you're sick?"

"What does being sick mean? Have you lost your intelligence so fast? I'm dying, Adesuwa, your father is sick. Brain tumor, Grade II glioma. Got diagnosed few weeks ago."

I must have been looking at him with fear and horror in my eyes because he broke into a playful laughter. "I'm not going to die so soon if that's what you think. I still have perhaps, a few years if given perfect treatment."

"You...have... Cancer?" I whispered, my voice shaky. His expression turned warm instantly as he smiled sadly at me. He didn't need to give an answer, it was all there, clear on his face.

"karma is a bitch right?" He chuckled lightly, his eyes looking too red rimmed. I felt so much pity for this man. This man who was my father.

"That is all the more reason why you shouldn't have come here. You need to rest, dad. You need to be treated so you can get better, not parade around the whole of Abuja looking for a daughter you don't even care about in the first place."

"I'm sorry..." His frail voice trailed off.

"It's okay. I need you to be on your way now, I have class right now and the sooner you get back to Lagos, the better for your health." I needed to shut him out before I let myself get hurt, once again.

My dad grimaced and pulled himself to stand in front of me. I stared at him and he stared at me. I tried to search for a single semblance of me in him. None. Our eyes were a different contrast, his were a light brown, almost close to Grey, mine was pure brown. His nose was pointed and a bit wide, mine was pointed and small. He's dark, I'm fair. Not too fair though.

"Take care of yourself, Adesuwa. I don't want to hear that anything bad happened to you."

"I will." I replied sharply. My mind still revisiting the news of his sickness.

We stared at each other for another while before I released an exasperated breath and pulled in him for a hug. I knew he was smiling from my back. I didn't let it enter 5 seconds before I pulled away quickly and said my goodbye.

"Oh, and before I forget," He reached into his pocket and pulled out a small, jewelry box and handed it over to me. "A friend of yours in lagos, asked me to drop this for you. Said her name is Adunni."

I frowned confusedly. The Adunni I remembered was hardly my friend anymore. She wasn't even my friend to begin with. She'd been one of the top girls in junior high school back in lagos, and she was always mean to me. Why would she have a gift for me? Years later?

"Alright, thank you." I collected it and dropped it on my bed stand. "I'll see you off as I'm on my way to class as well."

"You're just so eager for me to leave you alone. Let's sha go."

****

"Did you both fight a mortal combat? And I hope you were the one that won? Did you punch him in the face and say 'Daddy you're a weak, old man, you're no match for me!'"

I let out a laugh as Amarachi continued with her rants. We had just finished the program which had to do with the charity organization for the school, when Amara was asking me how it went down between me and my dad.

"Funnily enough, nothing went down. He was cool and we talked for a while..." I couldn't just break the news about my dad's health situation to her, even though I really wanted to.

"Remind me why you don't have a good relationship with your father again?" she questioned, her tone accusatory.

"Well...."

The sound of my phone stopped me and as I raised it up and saw that it was Richard calling, all other thoughts left my head. Finally.

"Richard... Hi..."

"I'm in front of your hostel. Come here Now."

What is it with the men in my life showing up at my hostel unannounced!

"We all can't get enough of you that's why." I hadn't realized that I had said that out loud until Amarachi replied.

"Come on! Let's go see your boyfriend!"

WHEN WE GOT TO MY HOSTEL, I saw Richard standing close to his car, with two other girls who looked like they were about to eat him up. Sucking in a harsh breath, I watched with jealousy as the girls gushed over my boyfriend. Why are you jealous? You're not supposed to be jealous! You're never jealous over any guy!

I was there, berating my self, not knowing my friend was laughing at me."Oh my God!" She said with laughter filled in her voice, making me blink in surprise. "You're so jealous your whole face is red with it!"

"Oh for Christ's sake! Just shut up. I don't even care what he does!" I knew I was lying to my self though.

Immediately Richard noticed us standing not too far away from him, he pushed the girls aside and started making his way towards us, hands in pockets as usual. I took in short, shallow pants as he got close to me. I was sure even Amarachi could hear my excitement from where I was standing. I sighed softly as I took a good look at his tall figure, with a mischievous smile on his lips. God.

I unconsciously took a step backward as he held me by the arm and pulled me softly into him. Before I could say a word, his head came down and his lips touched mine in a kiss that said: you're mine.

"Don't you ever remember that we're in public!" I whispered harshly immediately I pulled away. I loved the kiss and wanted more, but he wouldn't hear it from my mouth.

"I'll kiss you again if you keep complaining." His deep voice boomed in my ear.

I glared up at him before grabbing his hands and leading him upstairs, Amarachi following behind. I didn't fail to notice the angry murmurs of the girls that he was with before. I smiled slightly. E choke them!.

"Why are you even here anyway? I thought you're supposed to be miles away.. In Ghana??" I queried as soon as we all entered my room. Richard casually propped himself on my bed and picked up the box my father had left for me before leaving.

"Who gave you this?" Richard asked. He had a suspicious frown on his face.

"Um... Just a friend from home. She sent it to me." I grabbed it from him and was about to put it away when Amara stopped me.

"Open it nau, it looks like a proposal ring!" She said.

I sighed. Amarachi was too curious to know what was inside the box. I wasn't. Reluctantly, I started to open it. I tore off the nylon all over it and opened the box. There was a small, round bottle made of glass inside it. Weird.

"So it's not even a ring.. WHO be the mumu wey send this type of gift?" Amarachi was saying, when I noticed a small piece of paper stuck inside the bottle."Adunni sent a letter?" I whispered to myself as I hastily pulled the paper out of the bottle and opened it.

I've missed you too much princess. Heard you in Abuja. You can run princess.. But can you hide? :)   Godwin x.

Slowly, very slowly, like in a movie, the bottle slipped out of my hand and crashed on the ground. But I didn't hear it. I didn't hear anything. Only a loud, loud, ringing in my ears. Kind of like the world was coming to an end. I tried to breath, but nothing came out. I tried to listen, but I couldn't hear anything.

Their voices, like an echo from far, far away was unrecognizable. I wanted to say something, but I couldn't react. I couldn't move. I stood in one place. It was as if time had stopped. Nothing was working. Not my head, or my heart.

"Sansa?"

"Sansa? Sansa! What's wrong?"

The devil from my past was back.

Chapter Fourteen

✳ Sansa*

THE FRESH MIDDAY SUN kissed my skin as I came to. While the weather last night had been dry and dusty, a cool and warm breeze softly greeted my body, making me sigh softly. I tilted my face up to direction of the sun, relishing the touch of the sun rays on my skin.

Slowly and reluctantly, I peeled my eyes open. Brightness. There was too much light. "Arrgh," I groaned. My throat felt like a sand desert. I needed water, right now.

Turning my head to the left hand side of the bed, I saw a glass full of water. Without a second thought, I reached for it and downed it in one long gulp. It was then I realized that I was not alone in this room. I turned and regarded the two men who were talking to each other in hushed voices, oblivious to my consciousness. Richard was staring at the other man who I guessed was a doctor or pharmacist, with a strange look on his face. He looked.. Helpless. He looked like he wanted to beg the man for a reason I couldn't fathom. I let an exasperated breath, alerting the both of them as they turned to me in shock.

Richard was the first person to react. He left the doctor's side and crouched right in front of me, close to the bed. I sighed as he gave me one of his rare, priceless smile.

"Sansa... You're finally awake. How are you feeling?" He asked, stroking my chin softly with his fingers. I had no other option but to smile sheepishly back at him.

"I'm.. Fine. Just a bit tired. And... Who's that man over there?" I asked, pointing my fingers to the man.

"He's a very close friend of mine and our family doctor. He came to check on how you were doing.. I suppose you're doing fine on your own, though" he finished with a bright smile. I felt my heart skip a bit, gazing at his overly handsome face. The man was a demigod.

"Why wouldn't I be fine?" I queried in a casual tone, frowning at him.

"Baby, you passed out yesterday.. After you..."

"Actually...I highly suggest we let her recuperate and gain more strength before bombarding her with questions and explanations." The doctor said, stopping Richard from saying more.

But he didn't need to say more. Everything came crashing back. My cheeks burned bright as I remembered everything that happened the night before. How I'd opened up the gift and found the sick letter from that sick guy. My throat closed up as I realized one fact. Godwin knows where I am. He'll come after me and try to hurt my friends as well as me. He'll hurt Richard. No!

I wouldn't be able to forgive myself if Richard got hurt because of me. Godwin was not just a dangerous person, he was the devil incarnate himself. A vile, wicked animal who loved to prey on people's weaknesses and even though I didn't wish to admit it, Richard was my weakness.

I stared up at him silently, tears gathering in my eyes as I thought about how he'd come to mean so much to me in such a short time. I didn't think I was capable of falling in love. I still couldn't grasp the meaning of love into my head, but I knew for a fact that I had deep feelings for this young man sitting in front of me, watching me as if I was one of his favorite movie.

"Sansa... Let me take care of you," He urged, his voice soft, mild. "Tell me what's wrong, I swear I'll make it right..."

I shook my head back and forth as I pulled out the covers from under me. I needed to get out of here. Luckily I was already dressed in a white jalamia I was sure was Richard's. I got up from the bed and took a step backwards as the force of my headache hit me.

"Argh..." I groaned as I felt Richard's hands circle my back area, stopping me from toppling over.

"Calm down, you fainted yesterday and you're barely on your feet yet you want to go where?" Richard demanded. I could trace the anger in his voice as he held on to me tight. I took a moment to savor the feeling of his arm wrapped warmly around my middle. That feeling of peace, of sweet butterflies dancing in my belly. I felt his soft breath fan the tiny hairs at the back of my neck. I didn't know when I would feel this way again. You need to do the right thing, Sansa. Push him away. He'll understand that you're just trying to protect him later.

With grim determination and whatever leftover strength I could gather, I pushed his hands off me with a scream that shocked both him and the doctor instantly.

"Let me go!" I yelled in front of his face. "Is it by force to dance to your tune??? You can't force everyone to want you just because you're used to getting what you want, Richard! I don't want you!" I screamed louder, tears streaming my face unbidden.

Richard turned to the doctor who quickly got the message and stepped out of the room without a word. Richard turned back to me and I could have died with the look I saw there in his eyes. The look of someone who was broken.

"Sansa.... I know something's wrong, you just have to tell me. I swear, I will do anything to make it better. Just tell me, please."

I shuddered as he pulled me into him. He kissed my cheeks softly, taking the tears away. I wished it was that simple.

"You don't know the things I could do for you, Sansa. I wouldn't hesitate to kill someone if I have to do it for your protection. Don't push me away, let me in, Sansa. Let me in."

Without warning, his lips crashed into mine with a rough fierceness that sent my nerves into a skyrocketing sea. I grabbed at his hair, his shirt, any scrap of skin I could find. The kiss deepened as he picked me up, setting my legs on each side of his thighs, his torso rubbing so sensually into me. My body felt like it was being lit on fire. We were sharing an incredibly passionate kiss and I didn't have a care in the world for anyone else. Only him and me. Locked into each other.

It was when my back hit the soft, warm bed I realized how far this had gone. My legs were wrapped tightly around Richard and he was straddled on top of me. I felt his lips brush past my chin, neck, over my chest that was vibrating Frantically. My nipples tightened painfully in anticipation of what was to come, how the buttons had come off to expose half of my upper body was beyond me, but I couldn't do anything to stop it.

I raised my head in a silent invitation as his head came down and his tongue circled one of my breasts.

"Ooh!" I let out a moan uncontrollably, trembling violently as waves of shock spiraled through my body. Goosebumps danced all over my body as if it was my body singing, and yes it was.

He quickly moved to the other one and circled his lips all over it. His tongue lashed and his teeth scrapped mercilessly. I was losing it and I didn't know how to control my self. In a bid to relieve myself of some pent up frustration, I reached up and ground myself hard into him shamelessly, feeling his thick, hard arousal pulse through my damp panties. Oh God...

I pulled at the rope on his sweatpants, ready to pull it off. I needed to feel him skin to skin....

We both froze in shock as the ring tone of a phone bursted all over the room. We stayed in place, him on top of me. The phone continued to ring out.

"Pick it!" I said harshly the moment I regained my senses and voice. Richard pulled away from me, giving me time to get myself together.

I jumped up instantly and fixed the upper buttons of my cloth. I was aware of how dark my eyes and cheeks were, but I couldn't hide the shame I was feeling. I had one job to do, push Richard away. Yet I was ready and eager to jump him.

"Sansa.." His voice came from behind me "I'm sorry about.."

"Don't." I said, my voice devoid of any emotion. "That was a mistake. Shouldn't have happened."

"You know what? You're a coward, Sansa Osaze. A big one at that." I met his angry, heated gaze. He was livid. "You kiss me like your life depends on it, then you call it a mistake. Is that how dishonest you are? You would deny yourself of your true feelings, just to validate some lies? What for!!"

"They are not lies! I don't love you, Richard Gentry. I'm attracted to you, yes. But I do not love you. You make me miserable. Meeting you was literally a mistake!"

"Falling in love with you was not and will never be a mistake." Richard said quietly. "I love you, Sansa. I don't want to think about what it would be like losing you. Don't you see?? You own me already."

I swallowed the whimper that threatened to come out silently. This guy was pouring his heart out to me and i was breaking it. Shattering it. I'm sorry.

"But I don't love you. I don't even like you.."

"That's not true."

"Yes it is! Just accept that not everyone will fall at your feet. I don't love you and I never will."

He sighed. "Sansa, if you're mad at me for some reason, please forgive me. Please baby, I will do anything for you to forgive me. Just..."

"You would really do anything to earn my forgiveness?" I demanded in a low voice.

"Yes."

"Then leave me alone. Stay the hell out of my life. Don't try to follow me, talk to me or beg me. Please."

He stared at me wordlessly, his eyes shining bright as he blinked severally. I couldn't believe I was making a grown man cry. I wanted to cry myself. This was all so pathetic.

"Alright." He nodded slowly. He sounded drained and I knew he truly was. "At least, let my driver see you safely home. Please."

I nodded slightly without turning back to look at him. If I did that, I wouldn't hesitate to lodge myself into his arms and tell him everything would be alright.

"Goodbye, Richard."

I didn't wait for a reply as I walked out of the room. Leaving him standing there, alone.

www.ingramcontent.com/pod-product-compliance
Lightning Source LLC
Chambersburg PA
CBHW070954080526
44587CB00015B/2304